I don't know any pastor who has been more personally fruitful in discipleship ministry than Randy Pope. Nor do I know of any church leader who has had a more sustained, lifelong commitment to making the ministry of discipleship as pervasive throughout his whole church. From this book you will learn both principles and practices for shaping people into Christlikeness by the Spirit's power.

— *Tim Keller, Redeemer Presbyterian Church, New York City*

Insourcing describes a pivotal change from latent repetition to active energy and individual discipleship. Step by step, you come to understand the progression and dynamism that has powered evangelical Christianity as the fastest growing social movement of the past quarter-century. You see through the eyes of one of its primary leaders and a great story teller. This is a book that every church leader (lay, like me, or clergy) should read.

— *Bob Buford, founder and chairman, Leadership Network; author,* Halftime *and* Finishing Well

I know of no pastor more willing than Randy Pope to examine his own successes to see if they cohere with gospel priorities. Randy's description of his journey from comfort in acclaim to confession of need for insight is as humbling as it is inspiring. I first read with a sense of personal conviction of my own failure to examine whether my ministry is about making true disciples, and then with a sense of eagerness to discover and do the kind of discipleship Randy describes.

— *Bryan Chapell, Chancellor, Covenant Theological Seminary*

INsourcing

The Leadership Network Innovation Series

Leadership ✕ Network
Innovation Series

LOCALLY MADE

INsourcing

Bringing Discipleship
Back to the Local Church

RANDY POPE

with KITTI MURRAY

ZONDERVAN®

ZONDERVAN.com/
AUTHORTRACKER
follow your favorite authors

ZONDERVAN

Insourcing
Copyright © 2013 by Randall P. Pope

This title is also available as a Zondervan ebook. Visit www.zondervan.com/ebooks.

Requests for information should be addressed to:

Zondervan, *Grand Rapids, Michigan 49530*

Library of Congress Cataloging-in-Publication Data

Pope, Randy.
    Insourcing : bringing discipleship back to the local church / Randy Pope
with Kitti Murray.
        p. cm.
    ISBN 978-0-310-49067-8 (softcover)
    1. Discipling (Christianity) I. Murray, Kitti. II. Title.
    BV4520.P58 2013
    253—dc23   2012037470

Published in association with the literary agency of Mark Sweeney and Associates,
Bonita Springs, Florida 34135.

Cover design: *Ron Huizinga*
Cover photo: *iStockphoto / Mark Wragg*
Interior design: *Matthew Van Zomeren*

Printed in the United States of America

13 14 15 16 17 /DCI/ 20 19 18 17 16 15 14 13 12 11 10 9 8 7 6 5 4 3 2 1

Dedicated to my children,
Matt, Rachael, Dena, and David,
and to their children,
Eden, Elle, Ford, Payton, Drew, Eason,
Luke, Ryanne, Wyatt, and those yet to come.
May life-on-life missional discipleship
be a part of your heritage and your lifestyle.

Contents

Foreword

It is a great honor and privilege to highly recommend this book to you.

I recommend it *not* because I know Randy Pope personally and have watched up close (in my seven years in Atlanta) the reality and impact of what you are about to read.

I don't even recommend it because it's a practical, helpful, and proven method for producing mature, godly followers of Jesus Christ.

Although those reasons would be more than enough to recommend it, I am compelled to offer the following three reasons you should read, digest, and practice what Randy shares:

1. *Christianity is in crisis.* Most Christians simply do not live like Christians.
2. *Jesus said, "Make disciples."* Even our most successful churches and programs are not producing mature, godly, high-integrity followers of Christ who, in turn, lead others to Christ and make disciples.
3. *Life-on-life missional discipleship is what is missing.* And this book does not simply teach and inspire; it draws on biblical truth and a decades-long proven track record, and it shows you how.

Every pastor, church leader, small group leader, and parent will have no argument with the case Randy makes, but few are actually doing what's described in these pages.

There are no shortcuts. Discipling your children, your small group, or your flock requires clear priorities, a specific plan, and large doses of time and energy in the trenches with those you're called to equip to become mature followers of Jesus.

The good news: this book will do more than get you started. I've devoted the better half of my life and energy to "helping Christians live like Christians," and this book is a practical and grace-filled guide to that end.

Thank you, Randy, for "doing it" rather than telling us what ought to be done. This volume is a treasure to Christ's church and for all who long to present a bride unblemished and pure to our Savior.

—Chip Ingram, President and Teaching Pastor,
Living on the Edge; author, *True Spirituality:*
Becoming a Romans 12 Christian

Acknowledgments

As I think of those who should be credited for this book, I have to begin with a number of spiritual men who, when I was a young student, took me under their wing to disciple me and modeled the practices that I emulate to this day. Also, the few hundred men who were in my groups over the last forty-five years taught me more than I have taught them. Those men include my sons and my sons-in-law. I am forever indebted to them all.

This book would be far less helpful were it not for the contributions of Kitti Murray, who is uniquely gifted to take my written and spoken words and make them come to life. She is not only talented but also a delight to work with. And the staff who work with me in Life-on-Life Ministries at Perimeter were invaluable. Bill Wood was a volunteer editor, coworker, and support. Charles Hooper contributed indirectly through his insights and the charts he provided. My administrative assistant, Jackie Lucas, worked endlessly to make this book a reality.

I am also grateful for Ryan Pazdur, Andrew Rogers, and Brian Phipps at Zondervan for their encouragement, support, and direction.

Rob and Jodi Reichel, through their real-estate company on Hilton Head Island, graciously provided housing for me to write in.

And last, I have to thank my wonderful teammate and wife, Carol, for her love and support year in and year out for nearly forty years of marriage.

To each of these mentioned, thank you.

Introduction

It was a time of evaluation. Of my life. Of my family. Of the church I pastor. Anything and everything was up for grabs. With a pad of paper in my lap and a pencil in hand, I stared at a wall and asked myself questions: How healthy is our church? How well are we progressing? How faithful are our people?

All appeared to be going well. We were far from a shallow church. We were uncompromising on moral issues, we were growing rapidly, and there were frequent conversions. The work of Christ and the centrality of the gospel were primary. There seemed to be unity and harmony among our people. Articles were being written about us. A prominent author included Perimeter in his book about innovative churches. I should have been more than encouraged. But I wasn't. Something was missing, and I couldn't put my finger on it.

I stabbed a single dot on my pad of paper. I imagined the paper was the wall in front of me and my pen was an arrow shot aimlessly at it. I drew a circle around the dot, turning it into a perfect shot on the bull's-eye. I laughed to myself, thinking how foolish it would be to celebrate when your target is *determined* by your shot.

Then I realized I had identified the source of my unease.

We were being celebrated and applauded, held up as an example of innovation, but for all the wrong reasons. The accolades we'd received were not because we'd hit an appropriate target but because the distance we'd shot impressed people.

It dawned on me that we had failed as a church to identify our target.

I knew what our target should *not* be. Not our reputation, an ever-increasing budget, or even gospel-centered preaching or a high number of conversions. None of these are worthy targets in and of themselves. They might accrue to us if we hit the right target, but they should never be the target itself.

After a few moments, I had a clearer picture of the target we should have been aiming at all along. It wasn't a number, a building, a congregation, an ideal, or anything like what we had achieved to that point. The target was really the life of a single person. Our goal, as a church, was really to mobilize each individual for the benefit of the kingdom, to see people become engaged in God's story, a story that stretches into eternity. The church is made up of persons, one unique person after another, each of whose name is known in heaven and whose hairs are numbered by the God of that heaven.

I wasn't forgetting the glory of God as our chief end, I assure you. But we should not forget that it's the *people* of the church who glorify God and enjoy him forever, not the programs or structures or events. The target of our efforts as a church must be the people, each and every one of them. But what does that mean, practically? What does it mean to take aim at the individuals in our care? If our goal is to connect lives with the glory of God, what would a life look like if we achieved that goal?

My first answer to this question was pretty straightforward: we should develop into people who grow in their commitment to Jesus and in their knowledge of the Word. Sounds good, right? But that isn't good enough. After more time and thought, two words emerged: *mature* and *equipped*. One can grow in commitment to Jesus and in knowledge of the Word without being mature or equipped, but the inverse cannot be true. I knew that if we set our sights on the spiritual formation of our people, making their maturity and equipping our ultimate goal, we would cover all the bases. And that is the target that has shaped our ministry since that day.

I've since become focused on the words *mature* and *equipped*. Though there are no clear definitions of these words in Scripture, I decided to take my best shot at biblically describing what a mature, equipped person's life should look like. My description certainly is not perfect, but it was close enough to create a biblical target.

A mature and equipped believer is someone who

1. is living consistently under the control of the Holy Spirit, the direction of the Word of God, and the compelling love of Christ;
2. has discovered, developed, and is using their spiritual gifts;
3. has learned to effectively share their faith, while demonstrating a radical love that amazes those it touches;
4. gives evidence of being
   - a faithful member of God's church,
   - an effective manager of life, relationships, and resources,
   - a willing minister to others, including "the least of these," and
   - an available messenger to nonkingdom people; and
5. demonstrates a life characterized as
   - gospel driven,
   - worship focused,
   - morally pure,
   - evangelistically bold,
   - discipleship grounded,
   - family faithful, and
   - socially responsible.

I know what some of you are thinking: "And where is this king or queen of glory?" Keep in mind that no follower can be *fully* mature and equipped. It is fair to say, though, that if one of these characteristics is absent, then that person is not mature and equipped. For instance, what if someone scores high in all of the other areas but does not live under the direction of the Word of God? I would not consider that person mature. Consider the qualifications for elders and deacons in 1 Timothy and Titus. No one meets every qualification to perfection; everyone is stronger in certain areas, weaker in others. But most people would agree that the absence of just one of the virtues disqualifies an individual from those leadership roles.

Back to my time of evaluation.

As I looked at my description, deep down I knew we had a problem. Far too few people at Perimeter could be described as mature and equipped—certainly not a majority of them, or even a large minority! And worse yet, we had no plan to get people there.

So how would we hit the target? The quest for an answer to that question altered my life and radically changed the ministry of our church. What we learned, through trial and error, is the focus of this book. I hope that the story of our search and the things we discovered will be as much of a blessing to you as it has been for me and the church I pastor.

Models
The Marriage of Dream and Function

The South Portico of the White House gleams for a moment in the midday sun. And then, as I knew it would, a distant, ominous rumbling begins. A shadow falls, and I grip the arms of my seat. A spaceship hovers above the White House, eclipsing all natural light, and then—I didn't see this coming—a single laser shot descends like unbending lightning from the ship to the roof of the portico. Smoke pours from the upper windows of the White House. Mayhem ensues. If ever Will Smith needed a good reason to kick some slimy alien butt, this is it.

When I went to watch *Independence Day* at the movie theater, I knew that none of what I would see on the big screen would be true. But as I watched the movie, my chest tightening with a peculiar mixture of nationalistic grief and pride, the action on-screen seemed real. Samuel Taylor Coleridge called this ability to enter wholeheartedly into a fictional drama as if it is real life the "willing suspension of disbelief." But I didn't discard my disbelief without a little help. In *Independence Day*, the White House destruction scene took a week to plan, required forty explosive charges, and ended by blowing an elaborate ten-by-five-foot scale model to smithereens.[1] Someone went to a lot of trouble just to make a story come to life.

In the movies, many a drama owes its punch to a model. In a pivotal scene near the end of the movie *The Legend of Zorro*, a 1:4 scale model of a steam engine was, like the White House in *Independence Day*, blown to bits. I'm sure most viewers were too enthralled with the film to suspect that a real, life-size train wasn't involved.

It's ironic. When the model maker does his or her job well, no one realizes there is a model maker at all. That's something a model maker can never forget. The model is the ultimate servant. And when the model's service is over, having served both the storyteller and the story's audience, it ends up in the dumpster.

In architecture, models serve both the architect who designed the structure and the people who will live and work within its walls. Once the real building comes to life, the miniature one gathers dust in a storage room. Again, the model is a servant. It plays a very important role, but it gives itself away for its intended purpose.

Models marry dream to function. Months or even years before the first casting call for *Independence Day*, as the tale was just beginning to take shape, a screenwriter might have dreamed out loud, "Wouldn't it be cool if the aliens blew up the White House?" The model made the dream visible and, in the end, attainable. Or consider this: designers labored for years to figure out how to memorialize 9/11 on the site where the twin towers once stood in New York City. Eventually, a miniature version of their dream was placed on display at Ground Zero, making it available to three thousand visitors every day. The model not only provided one of many templates for the realization of the architect's vision; it inspired a hurting nation with hope.

The Pastor as a Model Maker

Dream and function. If you are a pastor or a church leader, you know what it means to live in the tension between these two.

You have a dream, a vision that you hope reflects the heart of the Architect, Jesus, the "author and perfecter of our faith" (Heb. 12:2). The dream shifts and sharpens over time, but if it's from God, it is big and daunting and over-the-top. It reaches out to encompass that overarching dream of believers everywhere: to glorify God and enjoy him forever. If you are a pastor or a leader, and you don't have a dream, it's time to get alone and ask God for one. Leaders need dreams.

And then there's function, the how-to that connects the big, noble dream to real, flawed people in real, limited time and space. That's where models come in. You can't realize a dream without one. If you have a God-given dream and a church that functions, there is a model somewhere in your thinking, even if you haven't clearly identified it. Maybe you've followed the prevailing trends. Or you've reinvented the wheel — again — and your church is forging its own path. Or you are a classicist who values the traditional ways. Whether you lead in broad strokes with a near disdain for planning or you are a meticulous detail person who draws flowcharts in your spare time, or you are somewhere in between, you are a ministerial model maker.

The question is, How effective is your ministry model? Is it a servant, a backdrop that slips into near invisibility behind the purpose and the people it serves? Or is it so unwieldy that you feel as if you are serving it and not the other way around? More important, does your model facilitate your dream? If your dream were distilled to the fundamental purpose of humanity — to glorify and enjoy God forever — does your model get you there?

And what kind of people does your ministry model serve? Is your model made to serve real people with real lives? Think really hard about that one. How effectively does your model help your people glorify and enjoy God? I'm not talking about just the one poster child who is a shining example of the dream. I'm talking about all of the individuals in your care.

These questions convince me that models matter.

This book is about a model I have tested for many years. For more than two decades, this model has served well both

> By the grace God has given me, I laid a foundation as an expert builder, and someone else is building on it. But each one should be careful how he builds.
>
> —*1 Corinthians 3:10*

the purpose and the people of Perimeter Church. Without this model, I might have given up pastoral ministry long ago. I call it the life-on-life model, and I will describe it in detail later in the book.

But first, let's review three models commonly employed by the church throughout the years.

A Little Backstory on Ministry Models

1. The Pastoral Model

I'll refer to the first model as the pastoral model. You probably think of it as the traditional model, the way you remember church. The pastoral model has served many different traditions. It is a model of ministry whose basic building blocks are a small, stable flock and a loving, multitalented, maintenance-oriented shepherd. Simple means of grace are emphasized, Sunday school classes are taught, churches grow mostly through births and shrink through deaths, and things don't change much. The pastoral model seemed to work well when the world was simpler and the gap between faith and culture was less wide.

When church leaders compare models, the pastoral model has taken the brunt of criticism. However, let me remind you of one of the benefits of this model. In its day, the pastoral model was virtually devoid of consumerism. In times past, the gap between what church members wanted and what they needed was relatively narrow. Most people didn't notice a difference between the two. Today the dichotomy between the wants and needs of churchgoers is as wide as a megachurch parking lot. What people want, they don't need, and what they need, they often don't want. No wonder church leaders are often stymied! There are reasons to question the pastoral model, but consumerism isn't one of them.

In the decades before the 1970s, the evangelical church seemed designed—indulge me in a little hindsight here—to preserve its moral, philosophical, and theological traditions. Just as the religious leaders of Jesus' day mistook the extrabiblical traditions that built up around the law for the law itself, the church mistook its cultural patterns for its truth and its code of behavior. That didn't make sense to many of us. Before a new model of church was born, pastors and leaders began to question the old one. Why wasn't it working? Was it effective in connecting the truth of the gospel to the people who had yet to embrace it? Was the church in its current model relevant? These questions led to the conviction that something had to change. And it did.

2. The Attractional Model

Slowly, but not systematically, church leaders took stock of the world around them—the unchurched and dechurched of today's culture—and decided to take a new tack to reach them: relevance. This gave rise to the second ministry model, which I call the attractional model. A new breed of Christians flocked to churches where the message, the music, and the method suited their tastes. Then the gospel, because it does what no model can do, took it from there and drew them in. Established churches advertised their traditional worship services alongside their contemporary ones. Often, because they couldn't adjust quickly or radically enough, many of the pastorally based churches waned as new ones cropped up and grew, sometimes merely by virtue of their newness. Although we wouldn't have called it attractional back then, Perimeter Church, the Atlanta church I have pastored since its birth in 1977, came of age in the midst of all this change. We understood the need to stay relevant to our context, and we worked hard to do so. Without planning to, we joined a few others as the harbingers of a new model of church. Over time we either maintained or reintroduced many of the positive components of the pastoral model, which served only to enrich the attractional focus we had come to embrace. We didn't discard the pastoral model; we fused it to the attractional. The result was a hybrid many churches have embraced: the pastoral/attractional model. What's surprising is how attractional some of the more pastoral features of a church are to outsiders, such as crisis counseling and hospital visitation.

I'm not a church historian. I'm just making some very broad observations based on my experience and the experiences of other pastors and leaders like me. There are some who say the attractional model has been around since Constantine, ever since the church had the means to create an actual place — a church building — to attract people to.[2] While attracting people from the outside in may have been the strategy of the church for centuries, the touchstone of the attractional model today isn't so much attraction as relevance. That's what made this model seem new to most of us. The desire to be relevant drove the church to fine-tune its marketability to the outside world. And that wasn't all bad.

The attractional model spoke the truth to a world that was one generation away from throwing the baby out with the bathwater. As a result, we regained a platform in our communities. We moved church from the fusty rummage sale bin to the fresh efficiency of an IKEA. We caught up with new forms of music, art, and architecture. We found our voice in a culture where voice matters more than ever before. But as models always do, this one gave us a new set of questions to ponder. We drew people in, but how were we going to push those same people out into the world? Seekers, those who might never have visited church otherwise, found inside our walls a place to go for answers. But what about everyone else? The cynics, outsiders, homeless, diseased, poor, oppressed, and abused didn't really fit. There's only so much relevance can do when it is limited to a meeting and a meeting place.

3. The Influential Model

And so, as it has over and over, the church adjusted. We began to look outside our four walls again, but this time we saw the world a little differently. First, we understood that while people need the gospel, they also need food, clothing, shelter, advocacy, education, healing, and dignity. Second, we realized we couldn't deliver those things without going out to where the people who need them live and work. Attracting people to us wasn't enough. In many churches, this shift from the attractional model to what I call the influential model has resulted in an explosion of action in our communities and beyond.

In his book *A New Kind of Big*, my friend and colleague Chip Sweney tells the story of how Perimeter Church took deliberate steps to become influential. We were well formed in head and heart, but our hand was underdeveloped. As we strengthened the hand of our ministry, we joined with other churches in our community who desired the same kind of change. We became less focused on our own church and more focused on the larger kingdom.

In his book *The Missional Renaissance*, Reggie McNeal suggests a new "scorecard" for the church, one that measures our effectiveness by our influential impact instead of the numbers we attract. I believe that God has placed churches in communities and cities where they can become blessings. So when I speak of influence, I am referring to the church that takes as one of its missions to become a blessing to the community and thus gains the opportunity to have influence in word and deed. The beauty of this model is that any church can use it. It doesn't matter if that church is attractional, pastoral, or, as we are, a blend of both models. It doesn't matter if the church is big or small or somewhere in between.

And Yet the Questions Persist

I've surveyed these models—the pastoral, the attractional, and the influential—for several reasons. First, the most recent models grew out of the church's response to a desperate need to shift its focus. I support these models as valid means for necessary change. Second, I am culpable for them to some degree. Perimeter

Church was birthed in the receding wake of the pastoral model. I believe, in today's parlance, I would be called an early adopter of the attractional and the influential models. (Although, if I'm not mistaken, that label generally applies to technology, and I'm definitely a bit behind the curve in that department.) Finally, although we support and participate in each model to some degree, I cannot help but consider the questions they provoke:

What if the pastoral/attractional model isn't enough? What if it stops short of the real, deep relevance the gospel was intended to have in every individual's life? What if, instead of being "in the world but not of it," we become of the world? What if church becomes hardly more than a gathering of cool people who listen to cool music and dress in cool clothes, our only distinction being the Christian label we wear? What if, in giving everything we have to be relevant, we forget to become more than that?

Is the influential model the answer to these questions? I think not, at least not in and of itself. This model prompts its own set of questions: What if the influential model begins and ends with do-goodism? What if we create another Red Cross or UNICEF with no real connection to the person of Christ? What if we mir-

The New Humanity

The Christian faith took root and flourished in an atmosphere almost entirely pagan, where cruelty and sexual immorality were taken for granted, where slavery and inferiority of women were almost universal, while superstition and rival religions with all kinds of bogus claims existed on every hand. With this pagan chaos the early Christians, by the power of God within them, lived lives as sons of God, demonstrating purity and honesty, patience and genuine love. They were pioneers of the new humanity.

—J. B. Phillips, *For This Day*

ror Mother Teresa's actions without any of Mother Teresa's character or faith? We can all think of at least one ministry gone sour because of the unhealthiness of its leadership. What if, in meeting the needs of the world, we expose the fact that we are no different from that world?

What if we do work that matters, but we don't matter? What if all we build is a model, something that bears the sheen of newness today until it is blown to pieces or shelved to gather dust tomorrow? And what if we become pioneers of nothing more than new models, stopping tragically short of the "new humanity" we were meant to instill in each and every generation that walks the earth?

These questions don't negate the value of the models. I consider it a privilege, perhaps even a historic one, to have led Perimeter Church on the crest of both waves, the hybrid pastoral/attractional and the influential. But I am convinced the reason these two models have served us well is that we have examined them closely all along the way, and when we saw a gap—a huge crevasse, it turns out—between them, we tried to fill it. The final model I will describe in this book was designed to bridge this gap. I am convinced that without its connective capacity, the other two models have the potential to become at best obsolete and at worst harmful.

Let me rephrase the questions posed above more alarmingly: What if the pastoral/attractional model of church produced an army of Christians who are consumeristic, shallow, and bland? And what if the influential model of church cranked out wild-eyed activists who do loving acts without the love that springs from spiritual maturity? What if the church marched on, resolutely doing many of the right things, but without being the right people?

The Other Model: Life-on-Life

Several years ago, a church marquee in the Atlanta suburbs proclaimed "The Church That Loves." I can't help but cringe at that kind of message—as if no one else loves quite like this one church, or, more arrogant, as if they took the love test and aced it. Neither assertion could possibly be true. And yet I realize how easily this book could sound a little like that marquee. I'm going to talk about something as basic to the Christian life as love, and yet it is something often neglected. Most church leaders will agree that what I propose is indispensable to the life of the church. But some will wonder if it's possible in today's church. They will dismiss it because it sets a bar that they think is too high. But I'm going to share my own story, and the story of Perimeter Church, as—pardon the marquee-like bravado—a beacon of hope. Yes, this model is imperative. And yes, it can be done.

As I introduce another model of church, I am also aware that we are neither the first to do it nor the only ones. That's why I hesitate to call it a new model. Because it isn't. The best ideas are both new *and* old. They are fresh enough to arrest us, to catch us off guard. But they are old enough to cause us to say, upon further reflection, "Oh, I knew that all along." If an idea is old enough to be rooted in ancient truth and new enough to startle us with its originality, it is probably worth our attention.

This model is public domain, like the words of an old hymn or the literature of antiquity. We call it the life-on-life model. This is the model the church must embrace if the people who come to Christ via the pastoral/attractional model and go out into the world via the influential model are to do so smelling of Jesus himself.[3] I'm not suggesting that pastors and leaders throw out the old models. We didn't. But I am suggesting we ask questions of them. And in the answers to these questions, I believe we will rediscover the life-on-life model, the one that functions as the missing link between the other two.

As I've mentioned, we questioned our own models at Perimeter. But our most important questions weren't sparked by the models at all. They had more to do with the people themselves. Because after the model has been relegated to the storage unit or the dumpster, the people will still be here. And so we asked, Were our people becoming the right people? Not just a few of them, but the majority of them? Did their lives glorify God? Were they qualitatively Christlike? Did they know how to make good, biblical, kingdom-centric decisions? What kind of wives, husbands, fathers, mothers, bosses, employees, and neighbors were they? Again, I'm not talking about the statistical outliers; I'm talking about the rule versus the exception. Were they attractive and missional? If not, what good were our models? We didn't just scrutinize the models; we examined the people the models were created to shape and serve, the people we were called to lead. And when we looked at the people, we were stunned by what we didn't see.

The pastoral/attractional and the influential models are not enough because they do not account adequately for real people. It is easy for them to miss the individual, and they do not include essential elements in the mechanism for individual change. The pastoral/attractional model gives expression to the dramatic nature of the gospel message. The influential model reminds us that our message is too large to contain inside the walls of our churches. These models have challenged the church to stretch its presence in the world to the epic proportions it was meant to have. But they leave out one key ingredient. And this ingredient, if omitted, will one day render the church tasteless, toothless, and the very thing we set out to avoid all those years ago: irrelevant.

Somehow, we must learn to take the broad message of the gospel and the wide mission of the church and deliver it person-by-person until our people are filled with it. Somehow, the church must possess an integrity that bridges the gap between its words and its people, between its sermons and the souls in its pews, between its programs and each person's life. If this kind of integrity matters to you at all, you'll want to hear about this life-on-life model. And when I tell you about it, you'll probably say, "I knew that all along."

Flawed Marksmanship
And a Missing Target

If you're going to take a shot, you first consider the target. Targets precede the rest of the story. Before the archer places arrow on string and raises the bow, before he traces the trajectory of the arrow in slow motion and wonders whether it will hit or miss, before the moment when the arrow lands, either wide of the mark or quivering with triumph in dead center, he must know how to get the arrow to the target accurately. We had determined our target. But the big question remained unanswered: How do we hit such a target?

Time to Tell the Elders

I introduced this book by telling you about a time I spent alone twenty-five years ago, a time when I identified a specific target for our church. Whenever I return from a time away, there is always a report time. Nine elders join me to make up our leadership team.

They represent a few hundred elders who, along with our staff, pastor our church. They always want to know what I did on my time away. New ideas? Spiritual insights? Future goals? This time they listened with interest as I shared my analogy of an arrow and a target. When all was said and done, they agreed with my conclusion regarding our church's need for a target. My description of the new target made sense. Their concern? That I had no idea how to hit that target.

By the night's end, they had left me with a commission. Find the answer. They offered all the resources necessary. Time away. Money. Just get the answer.

The problem was that I had no idea where to start. I knew of no church modeling such a solution. Looking for suggestions, I gathered a few of our key staff. I asked them, "Do you agree with my assessment of our church?"

"Yes, we do."

"Do you know the answer to our problem?"

Targets Matter

William Tell, a folk hero of Switzerland, understood the importance of targets as few men ever have. Early in the fourteenth century, William Tell defied the Austrian ruler, Hermann Gessler, refusing to bow before him. As punishment, Gessler declared that Tell and his son would be executed unless he could shoot an apple atop his young son's head. Tell, a famed marksman, split the apple with a bolt from his crossbow, saving his son and himself. The infant nation of Switzerland came of age because William Tell was willing to defy its oppressors and, when it became necessary, make one of the more daring and accurate shots known to man. Think a target doesn't matter? Just ask any Swiss citizen. Better yet, ask William Tell's son.

"No."

"Does anyone know where to go to find the answer?"

One staff member had a suggestion. "We do have a number of people meeting the description of a mature and equipped follower of Christ. Maybe we could make a list of those people and then go talk to them. Perhaps we will find a common pathway for reaching this target."

We began to write names. A lot of names. But it was still a small minority of our membership. Then someone said, "Wait! Do you see what I see?"

"What?" I asked.

"Look how many of the men on our list have been in your small group, Randy."

With that, I pushed back. After all, I'd had more theological training than most, as well as more experience leading small groups. I knew it wasn't because I picked the cream of the crop of our men. I didn't select leaders who were simply waiting to be released. To the contrary. The men in my groups I had either led to the Lord or picked up in their early stages of spiritual maturity. Many of these men had been moral messes. Now they were godly elders leading our ministry. I explained all of this to the group.

"I understand all of that," one staff member responded. "But what I want to know is this: Are you doing anything differently with your group than we are doing in our small groups?"

My answer was emphatic. "Yes. Without a doubt."

"Then what do you do with your guys?"

My answer to this question revealed to us "the big aha!"

Five Important Emphases

The staff listened as I described the content of a typical gathering of my group. I have to be honest. Prior to this time, I had no thoughtful plan. No list of priorities. No brilliant scheme. All I was doing was copying what others had done with me. My discipleship leaders (as we called them) had radically impacted my life. Imitating their leadership seemed to be similarly impacting the lives of the guys in my groups. So I merely described what that looked like. By the time I was done, I had described, in random order, five emphases. One of our staff later noted that reordering the list would create a memorable acronym: TEAMS.

Truth

The first emphasis is truth.

Jesus taught, "You will know the truth, and the truth will set you free" (John 8:32). But I never allow my small groups to turn into Bible studies.

Sound heretical?

Don't get me wrong. I am a professional Bible teacher; I love Bible study. But I can't afford to let our small group time turn into *only* a Bible study. Why? Because I want my guys to learn, not just to be taught. So I teach them how to study the Bible, then I give them texts to study. On their own! And they come back with questions, insights, or whatever is on their minds regarding the truth they've explored.

There's another reason not to let a group become a Bible study: there's not enough time to do Bible study and leave room for the other four emphases.

Equipping

The second emphasis is equipping.

The question I am most often asked is, What's the difference between equipping and truth? It's simple. Equipping is massaging the truth until it becomes understandable and usable.

Let me illustrate. Approximately a month after our group starts, I do an exercise to equip the guys for their time in daily personal worship. I teach them everything I think they need to know about such an experience. I even give them a specific plan to follow.

I leave them with an assignment to spend at least five days over the next week applying what they've learned. Typically, each group member is faithful and gives it a shot.

I know exactly what's going to happen at the following week's meeting. "Were you faithful to your assignment?" I always ask.

"Yes."

"How was it?"

"Pretty good."

My response is typically, "Just pretty good? Let's do it together. You watch me. I'll pull you in where possible, but mainly just observe."

I will watch the time and keep it to a maximum of twenty minutes. Though that's much shorter than my typical time in worship, I want to make a point. You don't have to have an hour to spend good time with the Lord.

When finished I'll ask, "What did you think?"

"That was neat," they'll say. "Wow, I like that."

Then I ask, "Did you see me do anything different from what you heard or read about last week?"

"No, not really."

"Then why such a different response?"

"I don't know, but now I understand."

The difference is that they've been equipped rather than merely taught. Equipping adds modeling, explaining, and asking questions. It's massaging the truth until it becomes understandable and usable. It's what we call adding life-on-life into the discipling process.

I once heard an old Chinese proverb: "What I hear, I forget. What I see, I remember. What I do, I know." Now it's time to assign them the task of doing, having first heard and seen. The likelihood has greatly increased that they will now know.

Obviously it is easy to equip people for a practical activity such as personal worship. But you can equip people, not just teach them, in every subject imaginable. What about the biblical doctrine of suffering? Or an attribute of God? Or a biblical understanding of the gospel?

Believe it or not, equipping can take place in these subjects. But you have to learn to ask questions. To prod to see if there is understanding. Massage the truth until, as the leader, you perceive it's now becoming understood and usable in the disciple's life.

Accountability

The third emphasis is accountability.

Accountability is a controversial word, almost vulgar in some grace-oriented theological circles. And in some respects, that's an appropriate reaction.

Accountability can be either a helpful emphasis or a dangerous one. In a theological environment devoid of an appropriate understanding of grace, accountability invites behaviorism. But with a healthy theological perspective, it becomes the believer's friend, though even then, one must understand the design of accountability.

Accountability is often described as asking hard questions and challenging bad behavior. But accountability is more than this. It's the "one anothering" of Scripture, a brother or sister in Christ helping a spiritual sibling find "the sin beneath the sin."

Let me illustrate. Recently, I asked one of the members of our group a fairly direct question. He answered honestly. He invited the group into a messy closet within his heart. He explained that he had reverted to using the vulgar language he had used before he began an intimate walk with the Lord and entered our group.

I began to explore by simply asking, "Why? Why do you think you are using such language?"

"Because I'm angry."

"Angry with whom?"

"My wife and my employees."

"Why are you angry with them?"

"Because they don't do what I tell them to do."

"Why do you think you get angry when they don't do as you say?"

"Because I think I'm the king!"

Wow. I was a bit taken aback by his response. So I asked, "Why do you think you're the king?"

"Because of pride."

I think we found the sin beneath the sin.

The question became, What do we do with this newly identified sin? The answer was to repent, assuming he was willing. And he was.

This episode provided me with a perfect opportunity to both teach and equip my group regarding the meaning of repentance. I explained that repentance is not merely admitting to wrongdoing, though it certainly requires that. And I explained that it isn't enough to take the second step, being remorseful for the wrongdoing. As important as this is, it's not enough. Repentance isn't complete until one comes running back to the open and loving arms of our heavenly Father. It is coming to the realization that his love is enough.

After our brother indicated his desire to genuinely repent, we gathered around him. We laid our hands on him, and he prayed, and we prayed. It was an emotional moment. I think we learned more that day about accountability and repentance than we could have learned in a semester-long seminary course.

Mission

The fourth emphasis is mission.

Mission. Being "on mission." Going on a "mission trip." "Living missionally." What is meant by this word?

My use of the term has to do with taking on the mission of Jesus. Which was? To seek and to save the lost. How did he do it? By preaching and healing. We call it word and deed, explaining the gospel and meeting people's needs.

Where is this kind of mission to take place? Where we live, work, and play, yes, but we must not stop there. We also must keep in mind the need for believers to go to "the ends of the earth" (Acts 1:8).

In my opinion this is the most challenging of the five emphases. In a certain respect, it is "the lead domino" of spiritual formation. You know the game. Stand dominos up on end very close to one another in as long of a line as you please. All you have to do now is tip over the first. The others will fall as a result.

Take up the mission of Jesus and watch what happens to spiritual formation. I don't believe the reverse is true. Focusing on spiritual formation won't necessarily lead to our fulfilling the mission of Jesus.

I often explain this concept using an analogy. Assume I'm teaching a conference. I am responsible for structuring the use of the entire day. Partway through the day, I decide we will take a break. I invite each participant to a feast of delicious food. They eat until satisfied. Then I ask them to join me outside for an hour of exercise. I hear nothing but moans and groans. They have plenty of energy from the calories they've just consumed, but satisfying their hunger doesn't cause them to desire exercise.

But flip this around. If I have them exercise for an hour first, they will be ready to eat and drink.

The same is true of spiritual formation. In years past, I assumed that if I focused on the truth of the gospel and the means of grace, people would, as a byproduct, live missionally. Not always, if even often, is this the case. I'm amazed by how many gospel-focused, faithful preachers of the Word struggle to live missionally.

On the other hand, I've watched the opposite approach develop spiritually mature and equipped believers. I've consistently seen the men I disciple take up the mission of Jesus, and as a result, their hunger for the Word increases.

I tell the men I disciple to think of their mission as their exercise and the Word as their food. Both are essential, but mission drives nurture.

Supplication

The fifth emphasis is supplication.

Supplication is a synonym for prayer. I use it instead of *prayer* because TEAMP doesn't sound as good as TEAMS. The name is not important, but its practice is. We're talking about praying for each other and with each other.

During the supplication time in our group meetings, we learn how to pray, but we also learn why we pray. Most important, we experience the impact of prayer. Hopefully, in time, prayer becomes a routine part of each disciple's life. It becomes a means of drawing near not only to God but also to the others participating in the group.

Here's how we structure our supplication time, using the model of the Lord's Prayer:

God's honor. We spend time acknowledging God's worth. "Our Father in heaven, hallowed be your name."

God's kingdom. Next we acknowledge God's priority on earth and in our lives. "Your kingdom come, your will be done on earth as it is in heaven."

God's provision. We acknowledge God's trustworthiness and thank him for the specific, fresh ways he has demonstrated it. "Give us this day our daily bread."

God's forgiveness. Members of the group are not forced to openly repent, but as they interact with each other in prayer week after week, they learn to acknowledge their repentance. "And forgive us our debts, as we also forgive our debtors."

God's power. We acknowledge our dependence on God. "And deliver us from the evil one so that we may not be led into temptation."

The five emphases represented by the acronym TEAMS soon became the focus of many of our small groups, which we called Journey Groups. And we discovered that what had been taking place in my group was now being experienced by many groups. Leadership began to emerge as never before. Though it took several years, discipleship with a TEAMS emphasis gradually became part of our DNA. But we had no idea of the learning curve that was still ahead for us.

An "Aha!" Moment with Ken Blanchard

Many know Ken Blanchard as a business leader and the noted author of more than forty books, including *The One Minute Manager.* I was first introduced to Ken at a leadership forum for pastors, where about twenty of us spent three days picking his brain for insights to benefit our ministries. At that time, Ken was a brand-new follower of Christ.

One day someone asked, "Ken, what has made your business so extremely successful?"

Ken responded by explaining how his company and books were founded on what he calls his situational leadership paradigm. "Many years later," he said, "I came to understand how this paradigm was consistent with biblical truth." Years later, Ken launched a ministry known as Lead Like Jesus, which he founded on this reality.

For those who are unfamiliar with this paradigm, this is how he explained it. He first drew a box with four quadrants. He then filled in each quadrant with a word. (See fig. 1.)

He first placed the word *direct* in the lower left box. "Assume you take on a new employee," he said. "The first thing you must do is to give him directions. He needs to know what is expected. Where things are, how things operate." He noted that if you continue to offer only directives, you will fail as a leader.

He then wrote the word *coach* in the top left box. "Coaching," he explained, "is when you allow your employee to watch you perform his task before he's asked to do it. It's allowing him to ask you questions and then asking him questions to make certain he

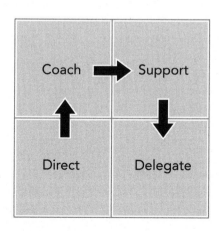

Figure 1

understands what he's being asked to do. It's giving him feedback as you watch him begin to perform his new job."

In the top right box, he wrote the word *support*, and he described an employer who is available when rare, unexpected, or unique issues arise that challenge a new employee. This leader is down the hall or is an email or a phone call away. The employee knows where to go when he can't overcome a new challenge on his own.

In the final box, the lower right corner, Ken wrote the word *delegate*. Now the new employee has the confidence, skill, and experience necessary to perform his job.

At this point, Ken said something that I will never forget. It was profound. He said, "What you never want to do is go from 'directing' to 'delegating.' When you do so, you produce disillusioned learners. And I know of no organization as notoriously guilty of producing disillusioned learners than the church."

Wow. How true! Here's the problem with the way churches are being led. Sermons, seminars, classes, et cetera are all venues for providing directives, and there is no problem with any of these as long as directing is followed by coaching and support. But you and I know that Ken is correct. The church has failed at this point. Think about witnessing. How many sermons or seminars have we heard about witnessing that concluded only by telling us to go do it? And some of us have been foolish enough to try it. Once!

The Story of a Disillusioned Learner

I was first instructed in sharing my faith when I was a young student attending a summer beach conference in Florida. Each day we attended morning sessions explaining how to share the "Four Spiritual Laws," a small tract explaining the gospel. We were carefully taught exactly how to go about it.

On the last day, we were encouraged to spend our afternoon, recreational beach time sharing our faith. It wasn't mandatory, so I chose not to do so. I'm an introvert. Going up to strangers on a beach is not my cup of tea.

But God had different plans. He used my conscience to speak to me, and I knew that bowing out would be disobedient. So I submitted.

But I did so with conditions. I told the Lord I would obey, but I asked that the person I talked to would be both younger and dumber than me. Neither, in my opinion, would be hard for God to arrange.

I walked down the beach looking for what I considered to be my victim. Then I spotted him. He definitely looked younger than me and not extremely bright.

As I approached him, my heart pounded. I told him I was taking a community survey and wondered if he had a few minutes to answer some questions. (So far I'm right on script.) To my disappointment, he seemed delighted to help me out.

After we exchanged names, I began the survey.

"Year in school?"

"Sophomore" was his reply.

Not good. I was a high school freshman. The first of my conditions was denied. But it was close enough.

"Name of school?"

His answer threw me a curve I couldn't hit. "Georgia Tech."

He was a sophomore in *college*. All I knew about Georgia Tech was its football heritage and its reputation as a school for smart people. Now I was undone. I just wanted out. But I continued the survey. Two questions remained.

"Do you feel the need for a more personal religious faith?"

Without pause, he said yes.

Now I was really getting nervous. The last part of the survey had me introduce the tract, explaining that there are four spiritual laws that help people discover such a faith. Then I asked, "Would you be interested in my sharing this booklet with you?" (I probably said it more like, "You wouldn't be interested in my sharing this booklet with you, would you?")

Once again, to my horror, he said yes. I couldn't have been more disappointed.

Though I was petrified, I remained faithful. My weeklong

training had emphasized, "Just read the tract word for word—every word. No sidebar explanations necessary." So I read. "Just as there are physical laws that govern the physical universe, so are there spiritual laws that govern the spiritual universe. Law One is God loves you and offers a wonderful plan for your life."

So far so good. But then the next words at the bottom of the page were copyright details. Was I to read those? I paused and then I froze. (Now you understand why it was a challenge to find someone dumber than me.) The pause turned into an hour. (At least it felt that way to me.) The longer I said nothing, the more my victim stared at me with a confused look.

Enough! I was out of there. I stood up, brushed off the sand, then said as if it were part of the script, "And there are three other laws in this booklet, and if you want to know what they are, you're going to have to read them on your own." And with that, I took off running down the beach. As I ran I prayed a very simple prayer. "Lord, I'll never do that again." The guy I talked to that day is perhaps the only person I don't want to meet in heaven, assuming he gets there in spite of me!

After that experience, there was little chance I would have much of a future in evangelism. Why? Because I was a disillusioned learner. I was given a directive and then delegated a task for which I was not adequately prepared. I needed to be coached. I needed someone to support me.

But guess what? I meet with people all the time to talk about Jesus. I most often bring the subject up. I see a lot of people come to Christ. What happened? Someone came into my life and convinced me that with some coaching and support, I could be effective at sharing my faith.

Though I was skeptical then, I'm not now, because now I know the power of coaching and support.

At the time I met Ken Blanchard, we were already using the TEAMS paradigm. As I heard his explanation, a light came on. He was talking about the same thing. As I looked at his chart, I noted that "direct" is, spiritually speaking, the same as "truth." "Coach" is the same as "equip." "Support" is the same as "accountability." And "delegate" is the same as "mission." Just add "supplication" and you've got the ministry version of the business model of "situational leadership." (See fig. 2.)

Then it became clear to me. Most every church I'd seen was basically a one-story church, directing and delegating. Since that day, it has been my passion to help churches add a second story to their ministries by emphasizing the importance of coaching and supporting as well.

TEAMS at One Hundred Feet Underwater

The TEAMS paradigm literally saved my life.

Several years ago I gave our son, Matt, a surprise gift for his high school graduation. I signed us both up for scuba diving lessons. Because of my busy schedule, we took private lessons. I also talked the instructor into frontloading the classroom time into the first half of the course. Instead of going to lectures, followed by practice in the pool, we did a self-study program and prepared to be tested on our head knowledge without having experience

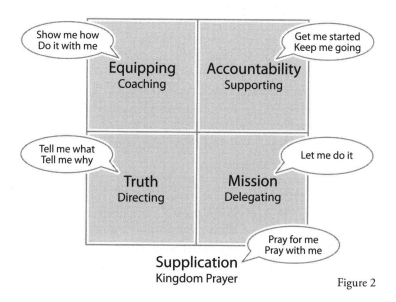

Figure 2

in the pool. Our teacher consented as long as we agreed to work hard and produce exceptional test scores. I figured it would be a cinch.

I studied diligently while on a trip to Asia. Even though I kept encountering words like *danger, life threatening,* and *serious injury,* I figured this sport simply involved jumping into the water and sucking air through a hose. How hard could that be? I learned that because water pressure changes at different depths, the diver must ascend slowly and at approximately thirty feet of depth must "hold" for three to five minutes to reestablish appropriate nitrogen levels in the body. Rushing immediately to the surface could be deadly. This warning, however, gave me only slight worry. I still thought the directions were clear, obvious, and simple.

Matt and I took our exams and passed easily. Now it was time to get wet!

First stop, the pool. We spent the first day getting acquainted with the diving equipment and practicing distress maneuvers. We then participated in our first role-play exercise as diving buddies. The teacher told us that once we were on the bottom of the pool, he would point to one of us to indicate which diver was "in distress." The victim diver would then remove the regulator from his mouth and give the distress signal (hands crossed above the head) and the out-of-air signal (a hand motion across the neck). Our instructor explained that there were a few vital rules for our time twelve feet below the surface. First, no one could abandon the mission. Second, the diver in distress could not grab the other diver's spare regulator. Instead, he was to wait for his partner to place it in his mouth, allow time to get stabilized, and then slowly proceed to the top. Simple.

Or maybe not. Once we settled a mere twelve feet down at the bottom, the instructor pointed to me. The calm I'd felt moments ago vanished. The signal came just as I had exhaled a long breath. I was already on empty. Without thinking, and before inhaling, I spit out my regulator. I then gave both signals to Matt, hoping he could tell I really was in distress.

If you know my son, you know he has never been in a hurry

a day in his life. As I slashed my hand across my neck, he seemed to glance my way casually. Zero alarm. He looked at his backup regulator as if to say, "Oh, I guess you need some air."

In my panic, I did the unpardonable. I reached out to seize Matt's backup regulator. The instructor slapped my hand away—rather rudely, I might add—so I did the next best thing. I began to swim to the surface. Just as I was about to reach the atmosphere, the instructor grabbed my legs and pulled me back down.

This didn't feel like role-playing anymore. It wasn't fun, and my lungs were about to explode. Finally, Matt was kind enough to give me his second regulator, and we returned to the surface.

After graciously chewing me out, my instructor explained how serious such a move would have been had we been one hundred feet below the surface. I shamefacedly agreed.

After that, you'd think the next lessons would be instilled with a certain gravitas. But no, I still figured this was all pretty easy stuff to master.

After more weeks of practice, we took a boat a few miles off the coast of Florida for our final deepwater dives and certification. After diving to thirty feet, then sixty, we got ready for the first of several dives to the lowest depth for amateur diving: one hundred feet. We rehearsed our plan to stay down for the allotted time and then at the instructor's signal to slowly ascend, holding for five minutes at thirty feet before surfacing.

At the end of our "bottom time" on this third dive, our instructor signaled us to begin our ascent. At approximately thirty feet, he gave us notice to hold. Though I fully intended to stop at thirty feet, I suddenly realized I couldn't control my ascent. In my inexperience, I didn't realize I had a pocket of air trapped in my vest. It was rocketing to the surface and taking me with it. Once again, my instructor found himself hanging onto my legs. This time he could only slow me down. As we broke the surface, we were lightheaded and grabbing our heads.

Once we were back on the boat, we evaluated what had happened. It was an unavoidable problem that rarely occurred, and it wasn't covered in the training manual.

We waited on the ship's deck while we accrued our "surface time," the required period between dives. Meanwhile, I was anxious about the upcoming fourth dive. My self-confidence was all but gone.

As we entered the water the fourth time, I was keenly aware of the instructor's location. I wanted him right next to me at all times. Dives four and five proceeded without trouble. By our last two dives, we chased fish with our spear guns, mindless of any fears or concerns. The dive instructor's proximity gradually became a nuisance. I was now sufficiently equipped.

I see the TEAMS process at every point in the training my son and I experienced. No one would consider going straight from the pool to one hundred feet in the ocean depths. It would be not only unwise but dangerous. My son and I gradually moved from the stage of directives (learning the "truth" about diving), to coaching (being "equipped" beneath the water), to support (my instructor offering the "accountability" I needed to provide security), to delegation (my instructor sending me into the deep on a diving "mission" accompanied by confidence based on experience). After this, the instructor was "prayerfully" available from a distance for further training, counsel, and delegation.

Diving without the instructor after that disastrous third dive would have been a nightmare. The "truth" I'd studied and been

Taking Aim

According to legend, William Tell had two arrows in his quiver that day in the square of his home village, Bürglen, Switzerland. If he had missed the apple on his son's head, the second arrow was intended for the man who had imposed the insane display of marksmanship in the first place: Hermann Gessler. Tell's story reminds us that no one wants to miss a target, especially the important ones. We can practice and learn from our mistakes, but in the end we don't shoot to miss.

tested on was nowhere near enough to equip me adequately. It did not negate my desperate need for coaching and accountability from my instructor. Yet this is exactly what the church is notorious for ignoring. We give our people truth and then delegate the mission of living for Christ without the necessary equipping and accountability. And when we do that, we're sunk.

Ready to Take Our First Shot

In our church we had identified our target *and* had a plan for hitting that target. More than twenty-five years ago, we aimed at a target we'd missed until then: the development of mature, equipped followers of Jesus. After eight years of rapid growth in our church, our people were not as near to that mark as they could have been. We missed the target because we didn't even know it was there. But once we had it in our sights, we were determined to hit it dead center. That's the rest of our story.

The Journey
Part One

The following is the fictional account of a discipleship group during its first six meetings together. At Perimeter, we call them Journey Groups, six to eight people who meet weekly for life-on-life missional discipleship. Each member signs a one-year covenant committing to the group. But the journey—the groups and the curriculum—can last up to three years, with some members rotating in or out each year. To offer a little variety, I have chosen to use a women's group for most of the examples. Later in the book you'll find the guys showing up in a meeting of another fictional group. The people depicted in these two groups are not real. These are composites of actual groups and actual people. And while these accounts can in no way reflect what really goes on week after week, they offer you a glimpse into what a group can do. Most groups go long and deep into the Word, into learning what it means to live obediently and missionally, and into prayer. These fictional accounts are simply pauses along the way to remind you that this book is not, at its heart, about a theory of discipleship. It's about the real thing: the disciples themselves.

"#!@#!" Billie looked up from her Bible. "Did you know it says that?" she said to no one in particular, as if startled that the five other women were still sitting there on the soft leather sofas in Lisa Mitchell's living room.

Donna grinned and nodded. "What is it about the 'story of glory' that surprises you so much, Billie?"

Donna had met Billie at Makepeace Elementary, where she tutored Billie's second grader after school on Tuesday afternoons. From the very first she couldn't help but notice her salty language, delivered in a crackly ex-smoker's voice that didn't match her youthful face. Billie's litany of swear words seemed to flow effortlessly, even when her children, who were three and seven, played within earshot. Before long Billie was a regular at Donna's table in her serene, empty-nester kitchen. Over morning coffee, the two women talked about marriage and children and friendships until, with nudges from Donna, the conversation led to an as-yet-undiscovered need in Billie's life for a relationship with her Creator. *I've rarely met someone so ready to meet Jesus,* Donna thought, *and so unlikely to fit in at a church, especially one in the suburbs of our Bible Belt city.* She was confident Billie would quit swearing eventually. Still, the habit was a rough edge she suspected might catch the others in the group off guard, like right now. Well, if their eyes weren't wide open to the Scripture a minute ago, they sure were now. As it turned out, Billie's enthusiasm was far less offensive than Donna expected. It was downright infectious. Now in Lisa's comfortable living room, Donna reveled in the joy of watching her friend encounter timeless truths for the very first time, truths that were in danger of seeming stale to the rest of them.

Just an hour ago Donna had opened the group in prayer. She would invite others to pray in the weeks to come, but she didn't know these women yet, didn't know who felt comfortable praying out loud and who didn't. She'd explained to the group that this first six weeks would be the toughest of their entire time together. Several of the women looked nervous, so she reassured them that that just meant doing more reading and listening to mp3s than they would later in the year. She encouraged them to persevere and quickly moved on to the next item on the agenda.

"Let's start the process of getting to know each other," she said, looking around at their eager faces, "by sharing our names and just a little about ourselves. Tell us your husband's name, if you're married, and the names and ages of your kids, if you have any. Also, tell us what you do—your occupation—and a hobby that you enjoy.

"Lisa, how about we start with you?"

"I'm Lisa," their host announced unnecessarily, "married to Tom, mother to Sam, who is sixteen going on thirty, and Bree, who is a freshman in college. I don't exactly work ..." She hesitated and looked around her own living room with its rich upholstery, original artwork on the walls, and antique Persian rugs scattered on the burnished wood floors. She then looked at the others, almost apologetically, and said, "I love to sew and I sometimes do projects for other women."

"I'll go next," Heather chimed in, almost cutting Lisa off. She was a petite brunette, muscular but feminine, with a tan that looked real, not sprayed on. She bristled with athletic energy. "I'm Heather. My husband is Mark and I have three kids: Carly is nine, Bethany is seven, and Josiah is four. I play tennis. Actually, I love tennis."

Heather's declaration ended abruptly. Donna looked at Billie and said, "Billie, why don't you go next?"

For the next few minutes, the women introduced themselves. Billie was married to David and had two little boys. She and her young family lived in an apartment complex not far from their church. Allison was a new mom with a streak of magenta in her jet-black hair and a delicate daisy tattoo on her ankle. She and Billie had discussed tattoos while putting cream in their coffee before the meeting began. Both Donna and Patricia were wives, mothers, and grandmothers who enjoyed reading fiction. It took some coaxing to get Patricia to offer this little shred of information. She'd showed up with her four-month-old grandson, Ethan, and a diaper bag. Patricia made less noise than her sleeping grandchild.

"Each week I'll ask two of you to share what we call your 'spiritual journey,' which you already filled out at the orientation," Donna said. "I'll start this week. I'm going to 'map' mine on this piece of paper."

Donna laid the legal pad across her lap and made one point on the far left side of the paper. "That's when I was born," she said as she drew a straight line about a third of the way across the page.

"When I was sixteen, I met Jesus Christ at a church youth group retreat," she explained, drawing another dot and then extending the line gradually upward.

"I grew some in my faith, but then when I went to college, my growth in the Lord really took off. I met with a group a lot like this one and learned what it means to follow Christ. From then on, I've had ups and downs, but the overall effect has been growth."

Donna drew the roller-coaster line up and up that represented her walk with the Lord for more than thirty years. She couldn't help but notice how plain vanilla her story always seemed.

She handed the legal pad and pen to Allison. "Would you tell us about your journey, Allison, starting with the 'neutral' time before you knew Christ?"

"Sure thing," Allison said with refreshing confidence.

Donna had seen Allison at church, watched her interact with her husband and kids. She reminded Donna of her own daughters, enjoying a new marriage and new motherhood. "My father left my mother a month before I was born," Allison said matter-of-factly as she drew the dot that represented her birth. "And then my mother started with alcohol and graduated to hard-core drugs. My grandmother got custody of me before I was two, and she raised me."

Allison's story was strung together with one harrowing

event after another. In the middle of the train wreck that was her family life, a friend introduced her to Christ. She was thirteen, and she grabbed the lifeline of the gospel and had not let go since. Not when her mother reappeared in her life every now and then when she needed money. Not when her grandmother died during Allison's first year of college. Not even when a moral tailspin led to pregnancy and an abortion and a long struggle to forgive herself and accept the liberation of God's forgiveness. When Allison drew a roller-coaster line that began its upward trajectory her senior year in college, no one doubted that it was an accurate picture.

Donna thanked Allison for sharing so honestly. "Any questions about our stories?" Donna asked, even though she sensed that no one could formulate a question yet. They would know each other well enough to probe later. She reminded them that she would call on two more of them to share next week. Thanks to Allison's riveting story, the women were now all ears. Good thing, because Donna needed to stop and emphasize a few important things before opening up the discussion again.

"We're going to be covering several disciplines of the faith in these first six weeks," Donna said. She thought she saw a few women squirm. "Remember, we don't practice these disciplines in order to gain God's favor; that's something we already have in Christ. No, the disciplines are actually to be practiced in gratitude for God's favor and in order to help us grow in our relationship with him. Some of you are list-checker-offers; you actually enjoy being disciplined. But I want to ask you to do a heart evaluation as you begin to get these practices down. Make sure your motive is to know God better, not to gain his approval or the approval of others. For this reason, we call them grace disciplines."

Then, with Donna leading them, the group went over their first memory verse together. After a few of them had recited the verse, Lisa said, "Does anyone else have a problem with this? I don't know if it's my age or what, but I can't memorize at all!"

"At all?" Donna asked. "I know what you mean. It's not easy for me either. But I don't memorize to memorize. I memorize so that I can meditate on God's Word. I kind of think it's an advantage that it's so hard for me."

"What do you mean?" Lisa asked.

"Well, it means I have to replay the truth in my mind and say it out loud more often than someone who memorizes easily. It enables me to hear and understand the Word in a deeper way."

Lisa looked skeptical, but she said, "Okay, so I won't give up. Maybe this is a blessing in disguise. I'll let you know what I think in a few weeks."

Next, Donna collected the group covenants from Allison, Patricia, and Lisa. Billie and Heather had until next week to turn theirs in. They opened their Journey Guides to page four and discussed the passages in John 1 and Colossians 1. That's when Billie got their attention with a choice expletive.

"I always thought of the word *glory* as negative," Billie explained. "I had one aunt who went to church all the time. She was really old school, like, she was religious, but to me her Christianity always seemed so angry. I thought glory was only for God, like a scary force field around him, not ever something he would share with us. This is so %$#* cool!"

Later that night, Donna told her husband how dramatically the "story of glory" had unfolded in her group. She'd led many groups over the years. This one had certainly started with a bang. It usually took weeks before the women became comfortable enough to share a story as broken as Allison's. The truth usually seeped into their lives over time instead of startling any of them like it had Billie on the first day.

The discussion about God's glory—that we were designed for it, that we lost it, that it is the only thing that will satisfy us, that it belongs to God—ranged from Billie's contagious awe about God himself to Lisa's vulnerable statement about counterfeit glories: "I don't want to make my children my idol."

Her comment led into a discussion about the exchange of

glory in Romans 1:21–23, which led to the topic of repentance. Heather said, "Repentance just means stopping bad behavior."

Donna explained that repentance is a relational thing. It means coming back into the embrace of a loving Father.

"But you can't just keep on sinning, right?" Heather challenged.

Donna reminded herself that there was more to Heather than the woman whose blunt opinions seemed to hide her real soul. She assured Heather that they would get to that question and steered the group to the topic of prayer. She explained that prayer is important for a host of reasons. Primarily, it builds our relationship with God, but it also births in us a peace that you cannot find anywhere else, and, finally, it brings results.

"Prayer doesn't change God's mind," Donna said, "but God uses our prayers to make things happen."

"I don't get that," one of the women said.

"Neither do I," Donna admitted, "not completely. But I do know prayer is the way I relate to God, just as conversation builds my relationship with my husband or my friends."

Donna peeked at her watch and realized they were about out of time. She prayed a brief silent prayer to finish well. Then she led the group through the section on accountability, explaining that accountability is more than behavior modification.

"Before we pray at the end, I want to talk a little about mission in both word and in deed," Donna said, "because both aspects are vital. Mission simply means to get involved in the mission of Jesus, which was to preach and to heal. Over the course of this year, we'll learn about some tools to help you become strong in both expressions of mission. Most of you will be strong in one and weak in the other, but we can never neglect the one that is the bigger challenge—"

"I have a college friend who is a religious fanatic; I mean, she's really wacko," Allison broke in, "so the idea of witnessing scares me to death. I don't want to be like her!"

"I understand that fear," Donna said, "but we're going to

do mission in a way that is easy to grasp. And we're not talking about buttonholing strangers here. We'll talk about mission where we live, work, and play. Probably one of those three 'mission fields' will be the one you're most comfortable and effective in. Hang in there; you'll see."

Allison smiled and seemed to relax a little. Donna then directed the group to turn to page ten in the guide, where they had written their personal prayers about mission. She asked if a few of them would mind reading theirs out loud.

Allison said, "I might as well. Here it is: 'Aack!'" She held up the page for the women to see the word in big, bold letters, and they all laughed. "'Oh Lord,'" she continued, "'I need your help. I want to obey you—at least I'm pretty sure I do, but I am so afraid. Would you help me? And help everyone to be patient with me. Amen.'"

Lisa cleared her throat, and Donna simply nodded to her. Tears accumulated in Lisa's brown eyes and tracked down her perfectly made-up face as she prayed. "Lord, I need so much help; I'm a mess. I know no one would believe it, but I feel like a failure, especially as a mom. But I know being missional is important. I want to do it, I just don't know how. And I don't know if I have the energy or the motivation right now. Would you help me, please? Thank you, Lord. Amen."

Donna let the silence linger for a moment. "Thanks for being so honest, Lisa," she said.

As the meeting wound to a close, they went over the assignments for next week, and Heather offered to make copies and send emails of the roster they'd put together. Finally Donna began a time of prayer.

"This isn't compulsory," Donna reassured them all, "but if anyone would like to join in, just speak a one-sentence prayer as we go to the Lord together."

On the way home, Donna realized every single woman except Patricia had prayed out loud. Just a sentence each, but what sentences they were. One word showed up in each prayer: *help.*

"Yes, Lord," Donna said as she drove down the familiar streets of her own neighborhood, "thank you for your help today and for women who want what you readily give. Would you help me help them? Oh, and Lord, I don't know what's going on inside of Patricia, but you do. Would you help her to feel safe with us, and with you?"

CHAPTER
THREE

Step One
Where Does a Sin Addict Go for Help?

Ricardo was a dedicated dad of three on weekends, but suffered from a daily addiction to meth which threatened to destroy his health, professional success, and relationship with his children."

"Tiffany had given up on her dreams of a medical career, and was allowing her family to care for her four-year-old son in order to devote herself to her IV crystal meth addiction."

"Jeff couldn't give up on his thirty-cans-of-beer-per-day habit even though his health was failing, he had recently lost his wife, and his children were struggling to cope with the loss of their mother."[4]

Whatever happened to the "anonymous" in Alcoholics Anonymous? Reality TV has dragged a very real problem — addiction — out from under the rock of private shame where it has been hiding for generations. The face of addiction is a very public one now, one with a spotlight showing us every ugly scar and shadow. And we love it, both viewers and critics alike. *Intervention*, an A&E drama about addicts and their stories, has even won an Emmy.

I'd like to believe the best about most TV viewers out there. I'd like to think that people watch *Intervention* because of the hope it offers families of addicts, because of the real-life turnarounds that happen to people like Ricardo, Tiffany, and Jeff. I'm guessing the show is less about taking pleasure in the misfortunes of others and more about identification, because most of us have a personal connection to an addict. And when it comes to the person we love who is trapped in the undertow of drugs or alcohol, we're looking for any glimmer of hope we can find out there. If reality TV can give us some of that precious commodity, we're buying.

Perhaps the most stunning "reality" in the stories of Ricardo, Tiffany, and Jeff is the fact that each addict has a home, a family, and friends whose lives are intricately intertwined with theirs. Each addict's behavior has wreaked very real havoc in those lives as well as his or her own. TV is hard-pressed to depict that kind of devastation accurately. If you've been there, I'm sure you know. That's what makes intervention so costly to everyone involved. It is a huge risk.

Sure, the folks at *Intervention* give the addict more than exposure to millions of viewers. For the addict who responds to the intervention of family and friends on camera, there are therapists and treatment centers standing by who offer not only extensive rehab but "relapse prevention" and "trauma resolution." The show's producers know that if they are going to exploit addiction for entertainment and profit, they'd better be ready to tame the wild animal they've let out of the cage. But, again, if you know and love an addict, you know it's a lot more complex than any sixty-minute segment of a television show could ever make it seem. And a lot more heartbreaking.

Help for Addicts

He's been your closest friend for many years. He's avoided you from time to time in the past, but this is different. You suspect something is wrong, so you ask. "Don't know what you're talking about. Everything is good," is his only response. But for the next few weeks, you keep probing. You've seen this pattern in others before. It begins to add up in your mind. You decide to take a relational risk. You ask him, "Are you an alcoholic?"

Apparently you've crossed a line. "Absolutely not!" he responds. "Who do you think you are making such an accusation? I may drink too much from time to time, but there's no way I'm an alcoholic. I can stop drinking anytime I choose."

As his responsible behavior diminishes and his relational distance increases, you take one last personal risk to help your friend. "I'm asking one last time. I'm asking because I care. You are an alcoholic, aren't you?"

For whatever reason, he decides to let you into his struggle. "Okay. I admit I'm probably an alcoholic. But I want you to know it's over. I can stop. I will stop. I'm through with alcohol forever. Never again will I drink. I know what it's doing to me, and I vow to you now, never again."

Let's assume that you have to bet your life savings on whether he will drink again. Where will you place your money? There's no debate. You know he'll be drinking again sooner rather than later.

Assume that he does revert to his former drinking behavior and, frustrated with his failure, asks you for help and counsel. What will you tell him?

Perhaps you would encourage him to go to a detox facility. You know that the cleansing he needs requires medical assistance and in-house counseling. You recommend a leading alcohol rehab center. Your friend agrees to admit himself.

Three months elapse and you get the first phone call your friend makes upon checking out of rehab. "I'm out and I'm free of my addiction! I have no desire for alcohol. I can tell you without question that I'll never drink again."

So what do you think? Assume the bet is back on. Same money on the line. Do you bet on his staying sober or expect a relapse in the near future?

If you know statistical data about the chance of relapse, you'll bet against your friend. Though you know he's sincere, a clinical cleansing is likely not going to suffice. Something more is needed.

The same is true for sin addicts. (And I'm referring to every human being.) At the fall, man lost his moral ability (not his natural ability). Though he can still do the right thing, he can't do it for the right reasons. Thus Paul can say in Romans 3, "There is no one righteous, not even one" (v. 10). "There is no one who does good, not even one" (v. 12). Man is conceived in sin (Ps. 51:5).

But it gets even worse. Sinful man is controlled by the influence of three forces: the world, the devil, and the flesh. Paul explains this in Ephesians 2:1–3: "As for you, you were dead in your transgressions and sins, in which you used to live when you followed the ways of this world and of the ruler of the kingdom of the air, the spirit who is now at work in those who are disobedient. All of us also lived among them at one time, gratifying the cravings of our sinful nature and following its desires and thoughts. Like the rest, we were by nature objects of wrath."

Paul's words to describe this "addiction to sin" are "dead in your transgressions and sins." In verse 2, he describes such an addiction as following "the ways of this world." This simply means living without God's presence and purpose.

A second influence contributing to our addiction to sin is described in verse 2. It's "the ruler of the kingdom of the air." Air refers to "unseen power." This, of course, is Satan, who is "at work in those who are disobedient." The phrase "at work" carries the idea of energy, force, or power. No wonder humans, outside deliverance from their addictions, are in such bondage to sin.

The last influence is referred to as "our sinful nature," or in some translations, "our flesh." The term has four common usages, two of which are used in our text: (1) that which is opposite of "spirit" and (2) the animal part of man. These suggest that humans in their fallen condition will find their cravings dictating their actions. Hunger, thirst, pleasure, sex, and desire to attract, though good in and of themselves, are not under our full control. Even the mind (fallen too) is controlled by pride, hate, and selfish ambition.

Humankind is in a moral mess! No wonder Paul concludes by describing sinners as "by nature objects of wrath." Not a pretty picture.

So back to our analogy of our alcoholic friend. He cannot expect to be helped until he is willing to admit his problem. So, too, with sinners. The first step toward cure is admission of guilt. Total admission.

A Friend Calls for Help

A close friend of mine, after being confronted with his alcoholism through a loving but hard intervention, immediately went to the airport to check in to an out-of-state treatment center. Several weeks into his treatment, he called me with a request. Would I visit him so I could gain some insight into how to support him after the completion of his stay? I was delighted to do so. I traveled to his treatment center to visit with him and to learn about addiction.

I'd heard about it, especially in a joking way: "Hi, I'm Jonathan, and I'm an alcoholic." Do people really say that? They did at the treatment center. Everyone's identity was wrapped up in the condition that forever will be their challenge. Even the doctor teaching our session on the medical side of addiction introduced himself by saying, "I'm Dr. Jones, and I'm an alcoholic." He'd been sober for decades but still knew the value of remembering his condition. Most addicts can quote the adage, "Once an alcoholic, always an alcoholic."

Christians would do well to follow their example. Perhaps when we meet in our groups, we should begin by saying, "Hi, I'm Randy, and I'm a sinner." Because the truth is, on this side of eternity, "Once a sinner, always a sinner."

Let's assume a sin addict admits to his sinful condition. What if he vows to quit sinning? Better not bet your money on him. One hundred out of one hundred sin addicts keep on sinning.

The sin addict's first step is to go for rehab. Cleansing. Where does one go for such help? Many would answer, "To church." However, cleansing happens only at the cross of Jesus Christ. He accepts us as we are—in our addiction, in bondage to our sin—and he cleanses us. He frees us from our addiction. As

Romans 6:2 says, "We died to sin; how can we live in it any longer?"

This is called the gospel, or good news. Many Christians claim to embrace the gospel, yet I wonder whether they really do. The gospel can be stated simply:

1. We lost it all.
2. He did it all.
3. We get it all.

By "we lost it all," I simply mean "we" (all humankind) lost it "all" (our perfection and everything else good) at the fall of our foreparents, Adam and Eve.

"He" refers to Jesus. He "did it all" by doing everything necessary for our salvation.

Then "we" (those who are his children) "get it all." We get everything necessary for our salvation and new spiritual life.

Sound good? Of course it does. But I think that many of us don't really believe this. Instead, we believe what I call "the distorted gospel":

1. We lost a lot.
2. He did a lot.
3. We get a lot.

By "we lost a lot," I mean we lost our perfection (which is a lot). But not everything. Because what we have left is our goodness. After all, isn't there a little good in everyone?

Most Christians believe so. Ask the typical church member what happens to a sweet fifteen-year-old girl in North Africa who dies in a car crash. Assume she had never heard the gospel and prayed faithfully to Allah as long as she could remember.

The answer will most often be preceded by some thoughtful stammering. Then the words, "I'm not sure. Help me with this one, Randy. I've always wondered how to answer such a question."

What they really are saying is, "I know that Jesus always taught that 'no one can come to the Father except by me.' But on the other hand, God wouldn't send a good girl like this to hell, would he?"

Interesting. We wouldn't have the same question about Osama bin Laden or Saddam Hussein or Adolf Hitler, even if they hadn't heard of Jesus. So why do we ask it about the girl? Because we believe she's good.

Not if she lost it all. Remember the text from Romans 3:12: "There is no one who does good, not even one." So maybe the Bible does teach that "we lost it all."

If we believe we lost a lot, we have to believe that Christ did a lot. He came to earth. He lived a perfect life. He died for sinners. But he didn't do everything. Why? Because we did something. We took the little bit of goodness left in us and created some faith and repentance. We did a little, and he did a lot.

The difference may not seem like a big deal until we come to the third statement, because if he did only a lot, we get only a lot. This makes the good news not quite so good. Though we do get forgiveness, heaven, and many other good things, there's something we don't get. His full righteousness. Why? Because we would have some of our own—thus, the good news is not good enough.

This distorted belief accounts for a church today that is filled, in large part, with Christians who perform to earn God's favor. It explains why moms who aborted their babies feel they are second-class spiritual citizens. It explains why so many of us expect trouble because we failed to spend time with God early that morning. It explains why the faithful follower cannot believe she is accepted by God.

After all, we only get a lot.

No, what we get is his full righteousness. The righteousness of Christ himself. Fully loved and accepted on the merit of Jesus alone.

Want to believe you got it all? Then you must begin embracing the reality that you lost it all and he did it all.

Just as our alcoholic friend benefits from the cleansing of his rehab, so sinners are cleansed by the work of Christ.

So if we're cleansed, no problem with sin, right? Wrong! Unlike our alcoholic friend who runs the risk of relapsing, sinners face the certainty of it. Every day is a struggle to obey. For some, it's worry. For others, it's selfishness or bitterness, misplaced priorities, idolatry, sexual disobedience, or poor stewardship.

An alcoholic needs more than cleansing to reach hopeful sobriety. Likewise, a sin addict needs more than cleansing to reach a place of healthy spiritual formation.

An Insightful Moment with Peter Drucker

Peter Drucker has been called "the father of management." He was a prolific author, famous business consultant, and graduate-school professor. I was blessed on several occasions to sit with this legend, gleaning from his wealth of knowledge and wisdom.

I gained great insight into discipleship when Drucker began talking about AA's success in dealing with alcoholics. As he talked about organizations working with people in the realm of social and behavioral change, he noted, "AA is only one of two such organizations I've ever seen work." The second is what he described as an effective church. He then went on to describe what I call "life-on-life laboring in the lives of a few."

Since that time, I've inquired into AA and similar organizations that work with people in addiction. My findings substantiated the insight I had with Drucker.

I've asked numerous recovering alcoholics why the recovery program they were in worked. The answer? Let me first take you back to the example of our alcoholic friend.

A Revisit with an Alcoholic

We left our friend with the reality that, by going to a treatment center, he may well be cleansed of the desire to drink. But statistics tell us our alcoholic friend most probably will relapse. So assume your friend asks, once again, for counsel. What advice would you give?

I would push my friend toward joining an AA group or, better yet, a Christ-centered group like Celebrate Recovery. Assume your friend enrolls in such a group and faithfully participates weekly for several years. Now you would be hard-pressed to know how to bet on whether your friend will relapse.

Why do AA-type recovery organizations work? When I asked numerous recovering addicts to help me understand the reason for their success, the answer was twofold: "We have an accountability group and a qualified sponsor."

Recovery groups are life-on-life. They provide coaching and support—everything needed to prepare someone for the delegated responsibility of living in sobriety.

The same is true spiritually: everyone needs a group, and everyone needs a sponsor. As we will see later, it's the way of Jesus and his twelve disciples. Jesus was the sponsor and the Twelve were an accountability group.

So we have to wonder why so few churches are making such an offer.

The Sponsor as Trainer

Let's use an analogy that might strike closer to home. Your doctor looks at you after your yearly checkup and says, "Time for some changes. Your blood pressure is too high. Cholesterol too. And while we're talking about high, your weight needs to come down quite a bit."

If your doctor is wise, he'll recommend, among other things, an exercise regimen. So now let's say you come to my gym. I explain that I'm leaving town for an entire year, but I give you a key to the gym, along with detailed instructions for every machine and a detailed written exercise plan. When I return in one year, what do you suppose I find? Lots of dust on my exercise equipment, that's what. And very little improvement in your overall physical condition.

But consider another scenario. Assume I not only own the gym but I'm a fitness trainer as well. And I'm not leaving town. I tell you to gather a handful of people you enjoy being with, and I ask you to show up with them twice a week. During our first meeting, I take you through a rigorous — but doable — regimen of cardio and strength training. I explain that you'll be sore the next day, but not so sore that you can't come back later that week. We meet regularly with your crew of friends. I give you instructions for how to exercise effectively on your own a few other days a week. I also explain that if you don't follow this plan, you cannot expect results. Nor can you expect to continue in the group.

If you follow this second plan, what would be the outcome after one year? You'd be fit and healthy, wouldn't you? Having a trainer meet with you regularly in the company of a few supportive friends could make the difference between physical wellness and physical decline.

There is no doubt that our physical health benefits from the ongoing encouragement of an athletic trainer. Likewise, our spiritual health needs the ongoing encouragement and guidance of a trainer.

Just as an addict needs the slow, methodical influence of a sponsor and others to get him or her to a place of hopeful sobriety, the cleansed believer needs the same relational process to transport him or her to a place of healthy spiritual formation.

When these types of relationships are in place, there is less chance of moral relapse, and the believer is willing to take the steps necessary for obedience. These slow steps toward maturity and equipping do not create overnight success stories. I know mine wasn't. When a life changes in this way, God's grace and glory don't manifest themselves in a road to Damascus experience, in a blinding flash of light. Something far more dramatic happens. God's grace and glory unfold in the course of everyday life.

In the following chapter, I will examine the scriptural roots of the life-on-life model of missional discipleship. But first I want to address issues raised by some church leaders.

First of all, the word *discipleship* can be confusing, if not misleading. I realize the word can have shades of meaning different from the one I propose. When words are this multifaceted, especially biblical words,[5] there is room for misunderstanding. Let me clarify what I mean by the word *discipleship* in the life-on-life model:

- The first component of discipleship involves helping people get from *unbelief* to *belief.* Personal evangelism and public preaching qualify as this kind of discipleship.
- The next stage involves coaching a new follower to move from *belief* to *maturity.* Small group Bible studies, Sunday school classes, seminars, and sermons can be effective, though limited, means to lead a new believer toward spiritual maturity. The life-on-life dimension of discipleship has the potential to bring about a deeper, longer-lasting maturity.
- The life-on-life model doesn't end with the personal maturity of the believer. The process of equipping moves a follower from *maturity* to *leadership.*

Life-on-life missional discipleship involves all three of these aspects of discipleship. And while I believe LOLMD is a more comprehensive, complete rendering of the process of discipleship, it is not the only definition. Therefore (and I can't stress this enough) I do not assert that the preaching of the Word from a pulpit or in a classroom is not discipleship. By definition, any way we help people to follow Christ is discipleship. That's why, when I made that difficult assessment of our church twenty-five years ago, I did not believe we were failing completely in discipling our people. I just knew there was more to it, and I knew that the "more" would bring our people to a new level. I also knew that if we were to be effective at making mature and equipped followers of Christ, we would have to dive into this deeper definition of discipleship. From now on, whenever you read the phrase "life-on-life missional discipleship" or see the acronym LOLMD, know that it carries the full weight of this meaning.

Discipleship: Luxury or Necessity?

If you're a pastor, the phrase "life-on-life" might trip you up because you think it means "small groups." Like me and many of the pastors I talk with, you may be disillusioned with small groups, and for good reason. Perhaps your church has them or has had them in the past, and they just look like spiritual babysitting to you. You haven't seen them produce mature or equipped followers of Jesus. People do benefit from the community that develops in small groups, but often the benefits begin and end there. Some small groups have even been known to "go rogue" and siphon off church members. So why try that again?

Or maybe you're not that cynical. I talk with many pastors who say that small groups meet very real needs within their congregations. We have small groups at Perimeter that provide a relational context for prayer, Bible study, and caring. Your groups may be functioning well, but you find yourself wondering if they could accomplish more in the lives of your people.

If we look back over the course of recent church history, particularly here in the United States, it is apparent that somewhere along the way the church lost sight of the form of discipleship I am describing in this section. If you will allow me to use the language of business, in a sense pastors "outsourced" the task of producing mature and equipped followers of Christ. I am not so sure this was done intentionally, but it happened nonetheless. Parachurch ministries were organized to help fulfill the Great Commission and to develop disciples who reproduced themselves. These ministries stood in the gap and provided a valuable service for the kingdom.

However, as the title of this book implies, God is calling pastors, leaders, and churches to "insource" discipleship, producing mature and equipped followers of Christ in the context of the local church. Leaders need to remember the example and command of Jesus to "go and make disciples of all the nations." Insourcing is life-giving and will produce leaders who will become a blessing to your community.

Maybe you consider discipleship to be one of those luxuries reserved for parachurch leaders who don't have to maintain congregations, elders, deacons, buildings, weddings, funerals, and a presence in their communities. Those guys can specialize. But you? You simply can't afford it. You get it, you really do, but you are way too busy with the big picture to pour yourself into "the lives of a few." How on earth is that possible for today's pastor? You embrace the target. Your church gears its vision, its mission, and its programs toward maturing and equipping believers. You encourage your people to have Paul and Timothy relationships, to practice one-on-one or one-on-a-few discipleship. But you? Your staff and leaders? As a top priority for your entire church? Not possible.

Or perhaps you have a more pessimistic view. You're picturing the pushback you'll get if you so much as bring up discipleship. It would take a veritable act of insurrection to get discipleship done in your church. Too many things that matter to too many people wouldn't get done. You'd be accused of favoritism or ineffectiveness. In that marketing trifecta—affordability, accessibility, and attractiveness—LOLMD just doesn't make the grade. It wouldn't produce results quickly enough, and everyone would get impatient with you. Whatever your job description is, you're pretty sure this isn't in it. Discipleship as I've described it is just not possible.

I'm here to tell you that it is.

Regardless of how you view it, spiritual formation through life-on-life discipleship is one of those topics that will never go away. It's just too biblical. It may fall into your slim file of pastoral must-haves, or it may smell like a gimmick you'd rather pass up. It might belong in your box of dreams, the place where you put those pursuits you believe in with all your heart but just don't have time to do. Or, if you're really honest, it frightens you because it's too intimate. But I challenge you to dust off the tired familiarity or the revolutionary fervor the word *discipleship* provokes, and consider what it takes to practice LOLMD and what might happen when you do.

I submit to you that life-on-life discipleship is like air. You can't breathe without it. And we all know what happens when we can't breathe. This kind of discipleship is like photosynthesis or the alimentary canal—not flashy, but necessary for survival. It isn't sexy. It might not contribute programmatically to the liveliness of your worship service, but it is the best vehicle for sharing something Jesus had the audacity to offer each of his followers: life. And that kind of life produces livelier worshipers.

The Journey
Part Two

"Look at this!" Lisa said to Donna, waving her hands in the direction of the marble-topped island in her spacious kitchen. Donna had arrived early for their second meeting to help Lisa prepare.

Donna glanced at the stack of books. "Looks like you've done a lot of reading on parenting. I remember those days when I couldn't read enough."

"Those are just the books about middle-school kids!" Lisa sighed and shook her head. "Do you want to know the reason I joined this group?"

"Yes, I'd love to."

"Well, a few Sundays ago, I almost didn't make it from the parking lot into the church. Sam and Tom argued the whole way there. I mean, it was ugly. We ended up sitting near the back. I felt like we limped into church like a family of wounded animals. Wouldn't you know it? We sat behind the Murphys with their six children, all smiling and happy and just so ... so obedient.

"After the service, I went to the bathroom and saw one of those stall announcements for a father-son outing. I couldn't imagine Tom and Sam together like that. I was trying so hard not to cry in church! I saw Barbara Cash as I was leaving, and I just blurted out, 'Where do you go in this church if you don't have a perfect family?' She suggested I join a Journey Group. I must have looked skeptical because she insisted they weren't for perfect people at all. She actually called later and invited me to join one."

The doorbell rang before Donna could respond, but she decided to go to lunch with Lisa as soon as possible. She knew about the pain of imperfect families. Lisa was right. This group was exactly where she needed to be.

After praying, making announcements, collecting signed covenants, and listening as each woman recited her memory verse, Donna told the group, "There's an additional task I'd like for you to do this week. You'll find a spiritual assessment online, and I'd like you to print it out, complete it, and hand it in to me. I know it feels like yet another thing to do, but it's important. It's a self-evaluation that you'll do again at the end of our time together. Any questions?"

"What if I flunk it?" Billie asked with a nervous laugh.

"Oh, Billie, I was just about to say that none of us can forget that our performance is never, ever the means by which God accepts us. He 'passes' us because he loves us, not because we ace a test. The journey is about our relationship with him, not our ability to appease him.

"Speaking of a journey, Billie, do you mind sharing yours like Allison and I did last week?"

Billie drew a line from her early years as the child of two loving but unstable parents. They moved every year or two, including a season in the Peace Corps and a few months living on a sailboat in the Antilles. What sounded exotic to every other woman in the room had made Billie feel insecure and different from her peers during those times when she lived in a neighborhood and attended public school. She shared her longing to give her two children the kind of stable home she never had. When she met Donna at Makepeace Elementary, she saw something in her that was deeper than a circumstantial security. Billie admitted she was even excited about tethering her life to a set of rules that made sense. In a very short time, knowing Jesus had given her life an order and meaning she had never experienced before.

Donna smiled at her friend. "Thanks for sharing. Any questions for Billie?"

The room buzzed for a few minutes as Heather and Lisa and Allison asked about living on a sailboat and about how many schools she'd gone to. Donna was about to break in when Allison said, "I guess I can ask you more at our play date tomorrow."

"Sounds good." Billie beamed.

Donna was grateful to know that the two women who had kids the same ages were already connecting. "Okay, let's see … would anyone like to go next?"

"I will," Heather said. Her story was a lot like Donna's. She grew up in a Christian home and responded to the gospel early in her life. Donna knew Heather probably would face the typical "good girl" challenge, to keep her walk with the Lord fresh and to know she needed grace as badly as Billie did. There were no questions for Heather, but she didn't seem to mind.

The women spent time reviewing their memory verses together. Then they shared their thoughts and questions about the Scripture they'd studied during the week. Donna probed when she sensed that a question or comment had a deeper significance.

"I have a question for each of you," Donna said. "What is your greatest hindrance to personal prayer and time in the Word? Is it making the time meaningful? Or is it keeping it regular?"

Billie laughed and said, "I've never prayed until a few weeks ago. And I think I've only opened the Bible a couple of times in my entire life. So I don't know yet!"

Everyone laughed with her. Allison said, "Definitely establishing a routine is my problem."

"I have a quiet time every morning before the kids get up,"

Heather said, and Donna noticed that she said it without a hint of pride, "but sometimes it gets stale and dry."

"Well, until several months ago I would have said keeping it meaningful was my problem," Lisa said, "but lately it's been different. I guess that's good and bad. I need God so much that I hear what he has to say with sharper ears."

"That's me too," Patricia said so quietly they almost missed her. With her foot she nudged her grandson's baby carrier into a gentle rocking rhythm. "I think when we're desperate we are more attuned to him."

"Yes, I find that's true too," Donna said. "At any rate, we want you to both establish a routine *and* have intimate encounters with the Lord. These first six weeks we're majoring on the fundamentals. Why don't you go ahead and pull out your Twenty-One Days of Worship. We're going to do day one together right now."

While the women found the loose-leaf page and a few got up to get more coffee, Donna added, "This tool is so important, we're going to make it a little more difficult. At least I hope it's difficult!"

"What do you mean?" Billie asked.

"Well, I want you to establish a habit, and it takes more than a few days here and there to do that. Notice this is called Twenty-One Days of Worship. That's because you're going to do it for twenty-one consecutive days."

"That's not so hard," Heather said.

"Well, for fun," Donna responded, "if you miss a day, just one day, you have to go back to day one and start over."

"Man!" Billie and Allison said in unison. They all laughed, but Patricia looked uncertain.

"I don't want you to fail," Donna said. "I just know that if you get to day eighteen and miss and have to go back to day one, you'll end up doing thirty-nine days! And that can be a good thing. Let me make it just a little easier for you. Pick a day out of every week that's your free pass. You just have to do six days a week that add up to twenty-one consecutive days.

How's that?"

"How about I go to Bath and Body Works and get a prize for whoever finishes first?" Heather suggested.

"Love it! Thanks," said Donna. "Now, let's get started. On your sheet, put today's date. What Scripture you choose to read each day is up to you, but I suggest we use something from *The Journey* curriculum. If you read a passage, like Matthew 6, just read until a verse or two strikes you. Today let's use our memory verse, Joshua 1:8, so write that where it says 'Text.'"

Donna explained that her goal was to model a time of personal worship to them so they could then go home and do it themselves. She glanced at her watch and said, "Okay, let's begin with prayer. I'm going to pray just as I might in the morning. Prayer is simply a conversation with God: 'Lord, would you be here with us this morning and make this a special time? My challenge is to do the right things with the right motivation, so I lay that before you and ask for your help. In Jesus' name, amen.'

"Let's continue and go through each short section together. What are your observations about Joshua 1:8? 'Do not let this Book of the Law depart from your mouth; meditate on it day and night, so that you may be careful to do everything written in it. Then you will be prosperous and successful.'"

"We're supposed to meditate on the Word all the time."

"If we do, we'll be successful."

"Great," Donna said, "now let's ask a few questions to help us understand the verse better. I wonder what the equivalent of 'the Book of the Law' is for us today. Any other questions?"

"What does success mean?" Lisa asked.

"Good," Donna said. "I wondered too. Now, let's interpret. Don't be intimidated by that word. We're having a personal time of worship, not doing Bible study. If we were studying the passage in depth, we might use commentaries or compare references, but for this kind of time, we use what we already know and what is already in the passage to answer our questions."

"So what is the Book of the Law for us?" Heather asked.

"I believe it's God's entire Word," said Donna, and several nodded in agreement.

"And success?" Patricia said.

"I think that means accomplishing God-given goals," Donna said.

"Like spending twenty-one days in worship," Allison said with a smile.

"Yes!" said Donna. "And the next section helps with that. Summarize specific and measurable applications of the text to your life. In other words, what are we going to do about it? The words *measurable* and *specific* are key. Today, I'd write, 'By God's grace I will begin today using the Scriptures to seek him for twenty-one days.' It's that simple."

Donna looked at her watch and asked, "How long did that just take?"

They all agreed that they'd spent just fifteen minutes. "See?" Donna said. "This is not as complicated or time-consuming as you thought it would be. And it would have taken less time if you'd been alone. That means we have time for prayer. We're going to use the prayer guide together."

Donna led them through a succession of prayer:

God's honor: acknowledging his worth, glory, and majesty.

"Our Father in heaven, hallowed is your name."

"I find I need to stimulate fresh thoughts about who God is in order to truly honor him," Donna said. "To do that I turn to the Psalms and read just a few verses until I can pluck out some reasons to praise God that day. Why don't we open to Psalm 3 and see what's there? Just read until you see something that describes God and call it out."

"He's a deliverer," Lisa said.

"He's a shield, a protector," Allison added.

"Oh! I understand this now," Billie said. "He's the God of glory!"

The women bowed their heads, and Donna directed them to voice their observations to the Lord in prayer. It was a short interlude, but they seemed to catch on to the idea that God's character was worth their verbal acknowledgment.

God's kingdom: acknowledging his priority in the world and in your life.

"Your kingdom come, your will be done on earth as it is in heaven."

"God's kingdom just means God's reign," Donna said. "His reign can be intensive, going deeper down into our lives. Or it can be extensive, going out into the world. I'm going to pray for both and you can join me if you'd like. 'Lord, would you be glorified in me as I go throughout the rest of my day? I lift up my friend Karen, who doesn't know you. I pray for my husband and my children and their families, that they would also honor you.' "

There was a comfortable, short silence and Donna was about to end when Billie said, "Lord, I want David to know you like I do. He thinks I'm crazy and he doesn't want me to pray with our boys. It's hard because I love him so much. I want him to find his own story of glory."

Billie stopped. Donna realized she was finished and said, "Amen."

"Billie, we all agreed with you in prayer. Remember last week I said prayer changes things? We'll all keep praying for God to change David's heart."

"Thanks, everyone," Billie said, her eyes glistening.

Again, the women paused to pray together. Donna felt like they were really catching the beauty and privilege of prayer.

God's provision: acknowledging his trustworthiness.

"Give us this day our daily bread."

"Praying for our daily needs is a way of saying we trust God, even if his answer is no or wait. The Bible tells us God cares for us, so we can cast our cares on him. Again, I'll pray and you can join in if you want."

Donna prayed for the activities of her day, for her neighbor's broken marriage (using first names only, of course), and for the weather for a weekend event at church. The other women added their own needs, daily things that mattered to them.

God's forgiveness: acknowledging your repentance.

"And forgive us our debts, as we also have forgiven our debtors."

Donna dove right into this one: "Lord, I repent of my selfishness. I know my desire to always be in control is an idol. I ask your forgiveness for that."

The room was quiet at first. And then Donna could hear someone sniffling, though she couldn't tell who.

"Lord," Heather said through tears, "I yelled at Bethany on the way to school. Forgive me for how impatient I am with her. Help me fix the damage when she gets home this afternoon."

"I was sarcastic with my mother on the phone yesterday," Allison said. "Forgive me for not taking the time to listen to her and for being so cold when she gets manipulative."

"I just don't trust you right now, Lord," said Lisa. "I'm scared to death of Sam being on the road, of Bree dating that guy at UGA, of Tom losing it with Sam. I just don't have much hope or faith. Forgive me."

"Lord, I guess I need to quit smoking weed," Billie said. "David isn't going to understand that either. But I know it's wrong and I want to obey. Forgive me. I have a feeling I'm going to be saying that a lot."

Donna allowed their words to settle and waited to make sure no one else—well, that would be Patricia—had anything to say before she said amen.

"Wow. That felt #!*@ awesome," Billie said.

"It sure did," Donna agreed.

God's power: acknowledging your dependence.

"And deliver us from the evil one so that we may not be led into temptation."

Donna explained that they would learn more about this last section of prayer soon, but for now she prayed, "Lord, I am reminded that I was lost and you found me. Your Holy Spirit now dwells within me. I present myself to you, my mind, my heart, my ears, my eyes, my mouth, all to you to use for your glory. Amen."

She had a lunch appointment to get to, so Donna was the first to leave. She was backing out of Lisa's drive when Patricia hurriedly walked out to her car and tapped on the window.

"Can we get together this week?" Patricia asked, so softly Donna could barely hear her over the hum of the engine. "I have something I want to tell you."

WDJD?

Where in the Bible Is the Life-on-Life Model?

If I were to wear a bracelet, mine would be a little different from the ones that were popular not too long ago. Instead of WWJD? (What Would Jesus Do?), mine would read WDJD? (What Did Jesus Do?). Sometimes the only way to answer the first question is through speculation. Any answer to the second question must rely on a study of the Scriptures. Though we often don't know what Jesus would do if he were here in our context, we can know what he actually did.

If I didn't already have a sense of wonder about his earthly ministry, I sure would develop one once I took a long look at what Jesus did day to day. To really look at his words and his actions in the Gospels can be a life-altering experience that leads to worship.

Before I make any observations about what Jesus did here on earth, I must underscore the truth that while he was here, he acted in perfect concert with the Father, that he is the one and only God-man, and that he—not us—is the standard of godliness. I also want to emphasize that the Scriptures are meant to be superimposed on our lives, rather than the opposite. We formulate truth for living based on the Word. But some things are hard for me to miss in the biblical account of Jesus' life.

Let's say you bought a red Jeep last week after a few weeks of researching a particular model online followed by a day or two test-driving them. You drive the Jeep off the lot, and suddenly it's like Jeeps have multiplied overnight. They're everywhere. You vaguely wonder if you bought into some subliminal marketing scheme to get 90 percent of car buyers to purchase the same vehicle. But in reality there are no more Jeeps out there than there were two days ago. You just looking at the road through a different lens.

Because it is our vehicle, I can't help but notice that our TEAMS approach to discipleship fits the life and ministry of Jesus as we find it described in the Word. No doubt about it, it's there. We'll be the first to admit that TEAMS is not a biblically scripted model; it's our model. It is our lens. Jesus didn't use TEAMS as his template for ministry. To be sure, what Jesus did during his earthly ministry went deeper and wider than our acronym. But I believe our template, although certainly not the first or the only or even the best means of discipling others, is a close derivative of the original. It's not complete. It's not perfect. It's not even unique. It's just close enough for us to know we're not doing our own thing. We're following in the footsteps of Jesus.

> *Truth*: At first, it seems everyone—lawyers, scribes, Pharisees, the sick and disabled, the parents of dying children, tax collectors, the disciples—called Jesus Teacher or Rabbi. According to Mark 6:34, Jesus taught the crowds because "he had compassion on them" and, in his estimation, "they were like sheep without a shepherd." But Jesus did not confine his teaching to the masses. His teaching narrowed at times so that the disciples got both additional clarity about his teachings and the full brunt of his challenges. He reserved time away with his inner circle of followers to dispense truth more completely. His disciples counted on him to interpret his enigmatic parables. In Matthew 13, Jesus "left the crowd and went into

the house. His disciples came to him and said, 'Explain to us the parable of the weeds in the field'" (v. 36). And again in Matthew 15:15, Peter asks, "Explain the parable to us." Truth was central to the relationship Jesus established with the Twelve, and he took great pains to translate it into usable form in their lives.

Equipping: In Matthew 10:5–8, Jesus sent his disciples out in pairs. The verbs he used in his instructions mirror his own ministry: "go," "preach," "heal the sick," "raise the dead," "cleanse the lepers," and "drive out demons." These verses tell us Jesus not only called the disciples to this task; he gave them the authority to carry it out. Add this authority to the months of living examples they had observed while in his company day in and day out, and it is clear Jesus went beyond teaching these men. He equipped them.

Accountability: Mark 6:30 offers a follow-up on this story: "The apostles gathered around Jesus and reported to him all they had done and taught." Not only did Jesus delegate tasks to his followers, he encouraged them to report back to him. As we know from the record of a failed healing attempt in Mark 9, this also included their "less than successful" outcomes. Of course, Jesus had a distinct advantage when it came to accountability. Even if the disciples didn't accurately share what had happened, Jesus "knew what they were thinking" (Luke 6:8). He could speak to their motives without asking a single question. There is no one else who can do this.

Mission: The mission Jesus gave his disciples was inherent in his ministry. By living his life in full view of the disciples, he readied them for the next step. During his last Passover with the Twelve, Jesus made it clear that truth isn't the only element of discipleship: "You call me 'Teacher' and 'Lord,' and rightly so, for that is what I am. Now that I, your Lord and Teacher, have washed your feet, you also should wash one another's feet. I have set you an example that you should do as I have done for you" (John 13:13–15). But Jesus gave the disciples more than his example; he gave them a crystal-clear edict, a commission. Nothing could be plainer than the now-familiar words Jesus used to send his followers on mission: "Therefore go and make disciples of all nations, baptizing them in the name of the Father and of the Son and of the Holy Spirit, and teaching them to obey everything I have commanded you. And surely I am with you always, to the very end of the age" (Matt. 28:19–20).

Supplication: Jesus taught his disciples to pray by modeling prayer for them. He invited them to join him in prayer, even up until the end, when several of his closest disciples joined him in the Garden of Gethsemane. And he taught them how to pray by giving them words to say, teaching them a language for prayer. It's doubtful the disciples called the prayer recorded in Matthew 6:9–13 "the Lord's Prayer," but they understood that the basic elements of prayer were all included in this example. Throughout their relationship, Jesus elevated prayer in such a way that Peter later prioritized it for leaders in the church: "[We] will give our attention to prayer" (Acts 6:4).

As we began to implement these biblical emphases in the ministries of our church, the elements we call TEAMS eventually became part of the DNA of discipleship at Perimeter. They have enabled the leaders to hold their groups to an appropriate, healthy standard, one modeled by the Master. The acronym wasn't the key, but the elements of it were. And when nutrient-packed seeds like these are planted into both the individuals and the culture of each group, they can't help but produce fruit.

Life-on-Life

Whether or not you see the acronym TEAMS in them, these descriptions of Jesus' life offer a vivid picture of purposeful discipleship. If we step back just a little from Jesus' day-to-day life, we can find additional Scriptures that allude to biblically rooted discipleship. I cite these references to point out the implicit — not necessarily explicit — biblical merit of the life-on-life model.

John 1:14 tells us, "The Word became flesh and made his dwelling among us. We have seen his glory, the glory of the One and Only, who came from the Father, full of grace and truth." We typically use this passage to defend the truth of the incarnation. But this verse goes far deeper than that. It uses the powerful words *glory, grace,* and *truth* to paint a picture of what Jesus' incarnational life on earth looked like. I believe many Christians experience anemic lives and do not healthfully reproduce themselves in the lives of others because they have failed to grasp the significance of these three words. The life-on-life model is designed to take people to a particular spiritual destination, one we have described as "mature and equipped." That's true. But we can never forget that maturing and equipping others in the context of incarnational life involves much more than a spiritual diet and exercise regimen. These three words remind us of the big picture — the final destinations in the discipleship journey. Glory takes us to Jesus. Grace takes us to the cross. Truth takes us to the Word of God.

Additionally, in John 15:1 – 5, Jesus gives us an analogy for his ministry that is bursting with life. Not only was Jesus' investment in others an investment of his life in theirs and theirs in his; it was designed to produce more life, to bear fruit. Jesus said to his disciples, "I am the true vine, and my Father is the gardener. He cuts off every branch in me that bears no fruit, while every branch that does bear fruit he prunes so that it will be even more fruitful. You are already clean because of the word I have spoken to you. Remain in me, and I will remain in you. No branch can bear fruit by itself; it must remain in the vine. Neither can you bear fruit unless you remain in me. I am the vine; you are the branches. If a man remains in me and I in him, he will bear much fruit; apart from me you can do nothing."

Watch what Jesus did with his disciples, life-on-life, and this organic template emerges. The vinedresser cares for the vine, prunes it when necessary, and waits for the advent of fruit. It's a beautiful picture of healthy spiritual growth — because real health produces fruit — at the hands of a skillful leader and caretaker.

Finally, we should consider a simple statement in Mark that distills the essence of Jesus' relationship with his disciples. I believe it captures the heart of the life-on-life model. In Mark 3:14, just before Mark lists the roll call of Jesus' twelve disciples, Mark tells us that Jesus appointed them "that they might be with him." Then he quickly adds another reason: "that he might send them out to preach." In this one verse, we see the marriage of God's pleasure with his purpose in calling his disciples. Jesus desired his disciples to be with him, life-on-life. That was his pleasure. But it was a pleasure with a purpose; he wanted them to do what he was doing: preach the Word of God. This reminds us that life-on-life is rooted in a relationship with Jesus, but it is completed by missionality. They are two sides of a single coin.

Doing the Same

One of our leaders summarized Jesus' life-on-life ministry this way: "Jesus did it, he had no other plan, and he commanded us to do the same." If the New Testament ended with the Gospels, we would get the message. But Scripture illustrates Jesus' mandate further by showing us the lives of other men and women who followed him, doing what he had done, just as he had taught them to live.

Even before Paul's conversion, the book of Acts gives us a picture of the disciples investing in the lives of others life-on-life. In chapter 4, they feed truth to others (vv. 8 – 12), but they don't stop there. They impart truth in the context of community. Verses 32 – 37 show us a group of people who "were one in heart and mind" and "shared everything they had."

The apostle Paul demonstrated life-on-life discipleship in his relationship with Barnabas and later with Timothy. In addition, Paul's letters reveal an intense focus on maturing and equipping others. Paul frequently mentions people by name, and he makes the goal of these relationships clear: "We proclaim him, admonishing and teaching everyone with all wisdom, so that we may present everyone perfect in Christ. To this end I labor, struggling with all his energy, which so powerfully works in me" (Col. 1:28–29). In his first letter to the Thessalonians, Paul describes the character of his discipleship relationships. He says that he cares for those he is teaching and discipling as a nursing mother tenderly cares for her child. He then adds, "We loved you so much that we were delighted to share with you not only the gospel of God but our lives as well" (1 Thess. 2:8). Paul was not content to run people through a program or a course of study. He loved them. He invested in them. He did exactly what Jesus did.

The life-on-life model of discipleship isn't the newest thing out there. One of our leaders recently commented that the challenge isn't to do something new; it is "to do old things with new people." Because this pathway to spiritual maturity begins and ends with Jesus, with both his example and his work of redemption in our lives, that's exactly what it is: an ancient way, traversed by people who have been and are being made new.

An Apologetic for Healthy Impact

Instead of Success

I drive a Honda, and I'm fine with that. I'm not trying to make a statement about pastoral excess or environmental responsibility. I'm just not a car guy. But I know plenty of men who are, who lose themselves in the presence of flashy automobiles. If they're idling by one at a red light or catch a glimpse of one out on the road, they can't help it; they gawk a little. They read the magazines and go to the trade shows. And these guys tell me you can't get much flashier or faster than the Porsche Cayman S. They say it can reach 62 mph in just 5.2 seconds. It has an alloy engine and a dual-mass flywheel, whatever that means. Although I may be unique in that I'm immune to its charms, for most men there's something about a European sports car, especially one painted "speed yellow" or "macadamia metallic," that catches the eye and brings out the Hot Wheels–collecting boy in them.

We started this book talking about models, but perhaps a better word for what we are describing here might be *vehicle*, because the value of a vehicle lies in how well it gets its driver and passengers from where they are to where they want to be. The Porsche

Cayman can sure do that, and then some. It has more power, speed, design ingenuity, and sheer pizzazz than any car *I've* ever owned. At least that's what they tell me.

You may be thinking I am now going to compare discipleship to a sleek Porsche Cayman S. Think again.

Are We There Yet?

From the very beginning, when we isolated discipleship as the primary variable necessary to the spiritual growth of our people at Perimeter, I was sold. We had been to the lot and we'd purchased the vehicle. But we'd yet to see what it could do on the open road. A vehicle that has not been test-driven isn't ready to be purchased ... yet.

And so, not much later, when I was invited, along with a dozen other pastors of large churches, to meet with one of the nation's best-known and highly respected pastors, I couldn't help but pack some questions about spiritual formation for the trip. We met at our host's church, a church that eclipsed all of ours in size and notoriety. Our host asked us to do something we'd done in meetings like this before. Each of us pitched our topics out loud and the leader wrote them on a whiteboard. Between us, we came up with twenty to thirty topics. I suggested we address the question, How does the church help its people form well spiritually? Our host then explained that he would use our first break to formulate a prioritized order for our discussion. Then after the break, he would talk for a few minutes about each subject, priming the pump for us to discuss it around the table. I was a little surprised no one else asked a question like mine, but I was still hopeful that we'd get to it early in our two days together.

After the first break, I looked for my topic on the board. There it was, dead last. I wondered if it would end up squeezed into a ten-minute time slot at the end or if it would fall off the agenda altogether. The longer we discussed other ideas, the more I assumed spiritual formation was not going to get its due this time around. But it did. With thirty minutes to spare, while many were checking their watches and thinking about shuttles to the airport, the convener said something like this: "As you can see, I left this topic until last. The reason is that I don't know what to say about this subject. In this day and age, how does a church significantly help its people in spiritual formation? If you can get your people to worship, do outreach, and volunteer weekly in a ministry, that's about the best you can expect."

I was stunned. *The best you can expect?*

Our host then asked, "How many of you had someone in your life, early on, who invested in you spiritually? Who loved you, but was tough on you like a spiritual drill sergeant?"

Every single one of us raised our hands.

"How would you do that now in today's church?" he asked. He then illustrated his point. He gestured toward a staff member of his church who had been observing the meetings from the back of the room. "How long have you been a Christian, Tom?"

"About four and a half years," Tom answered.

"How many verses of Scripture can you quote from memory?"

"Oh, about five or six, if you include the reference."

"See. That's what I'm talking about," our host responded.

Not that the number of verses memorized is a true measure of spiritual maturity, but what I heard him say that day was disheartening. A good vehicle is one that is created to move people from one place to the next, and then actually does what it was designed to do. Here's what this pastor's words implied that day, human visual aid and all: "We have absolutely no vehicle for getting our people from spiritual immaturity to maturity. We do not equip them. In fact, we cannot."

I'm afraid that pastor's words are representative of the church today. Listen to what George Barna has to say, based on current research about spiritual depth in church members:

> Four out of ten self-identified Christian adults (39%) have participated in a combination of three "normal" religious activities in the past week (i.e., attending church services, praying, reading the Bible). But far fewer have engaged in another trio of deeper faith expressions: less than one out of ten have talked

about their faith with a non-Christian, fasted for religious purposes, and had an extended time of spiritual reflection during the past week.[6]

Only one out of every five self-identified Christians (21%) believes that spiritual maturity requires a vital connection to a community of faith. Further, only one-third (35%) claims to have confessed their sins verbally to another believer at some point during the past quarter.[7]

All of this, in an era of "successful" churches that attract thousands to their services, their satellites, and their small-screen

The Sustainable Cycle

There's another vehicle I want to tell you about. It's called a Sustainable Cycle, and it's not much to look at, until you consider its purpose and how well it fulfills it. The cycle is the brainchild of a ministry with a heart and a calling to make a difference in Rwanda. Coffee bean growers there can buy one through a microfinance loan or a ministry gift. Sturdy enough to traverse a heavily rutted African road from the farmer's plot to the coffee-bean washing station and then to the market, the bike is genius on two wheels. Just $250 provides one of these specially designed bicycles to an African small business owner. That's nothing compared to the price tag on a Porsche Cayman, but the impact it can make on a business owner's life, on the life of his family, and on a struggling community is priceless. If a Porsche says success, a Sustainable Cycle says impact. And I'll take impact over success any day. (If you would like to read more about the impact of the Sustainable Cycle in Africa, check out *www.worldbicycle relief.org/pages/the-bike* and the microenterprise impact of the bicycle at *www.share5.org/2009/05/first-rwandan-sustainable-cycle-coffee-bikes-delivered/*.)

remote venues. Our ministry vehicles these days are veritable Porsches, fast enough to stream our live podcasts with lightning speed and flashy enough to wow audiences with our fog machines and cinematic lighting. By just about every measure of success, we're ahead of the curve. But what if success is not, nor ever has been, the most desirable destination of the church?

One danger of success is how apt we are to imitate it. You know the pattern. A church stuns its peers with some unprecedented practice or program. Other churches can't help but notice the splash. It looks like it works. Before you know it, everyone is doing the same thing. The end seems to justify the means. If it works (appears successful), give it a try.

If not success, what then is the goal of the church? Just as model marries dream to function, vehicle marries direction to destination. I think the examples of "disciples" that we find in the Old Testament give us a clue to this. The Scriptures are full of people who had an impact but who were decidedly unambitious. Joseph. Moses. Rahab. David. Daniel. Esther and her guardian, Mordecai. They obeyed God and, in doing so, impacted their communities and beyond. Were they successful? Sometimes. Were they bringing about healthy impact? Always. One need only download Jesus' Sermon on the Mount to see that the metrics of the kingdom are upside down compared with the rest of the world. Jesus gives us a taste of the unique flavor of kingdom values, and individual success is nowhere in the recipe: the poor are rich, the last are first, the hungry are full, the thirsty are satisfied, the persecuted are heirs. To the ambitious, this makes no sense at all.

If success is the byproduct of ambition, healthy impact is the byproduct of faithful obedience. This chapter isn't an apologetic for success; it is an apologetic for impact. If you want success, drive a Porsche. If you want healthy impact, ride a bike, as unlikely a vehicle as that may be.

Lively or Alive?

The Urban Dictionary calls them *successories*, those motivational phrases we shout from the sidelines, primarily at sporting events.

They are common utterances like "You can do it!" or "Eyes on the prize!" The funny thing about these successories is they don't always match the action on the field. There's nothing more discouraging than knowing that the team or the player you're cheering on with your words didn't practice enough or isn't naturally talented enough to live up to those words. In those cases, we're like Miracle Max in *The Princess Bride*, who yells, "Have fun stormin' the castle!" as the protagonists march off to save the princess. When his wife whispers, "Do you think it will work?" he says under his breath, "It'll take a miracle." You may not say it, but you know it. Your successories aren't always spoken in the context of reality.

Inspirational slogans like these may be fine for the playing field or fairy tales, but they have no place in the church. In the church, we have to be honest. In the church, we have to choose our words far more carefully. In the church, if we don't mean what we say and say what we mean, we run the risk of producing disillusioned learners or, worse, earning the disdain of a watching world. That's why the marquee and the website and, yes, even the sermon can be dangerous communication tools if we're not careful. We can say we're full of life when we're really just lively every time several hundred of us gather to sing. We can say we're cutting edge when all we have is a better web design than the guys down the street. We can say we're friendly when we splurge more often on coffee and doughnuts. These successories are a little like the images people project on Facebook. They simply don't reflect the truth.

To become a church of healthy impact, we need to dispense with the upbeat marketing taglines (unless they fit) and start by asking the hard questions instead. What is the purpose of the vehicles, or models, your church employs? Is it success, something that can be gauged by numbers and buildings and programs? Or is it impact, something that can be measured only by truthfully examining the lives of your people and the lives of the people they touch? Let's say you want to be a church of impact. Do you own a vehicle that can get you there? That's the question to ask first before even thinking about how to position your church in the community with relevant-sounding phrases or appealing imagery.

Ask the difficult questions that point to who you are as a church, not what you look like. And then keep asking them. If Christ, like salt, is meant to add flavor to the world, how are you doing? Are your people well marinated, tenderized, and tasty? How mature are they? How equipped are they to do the work of the kingdom? How often do you, the pastor or the leader, find yourself putting out fires because of their immaturity? Do you get sidetracked dealing with issues unrelated to the kingdom? How often does an initiative falter or fail because those who are involved in it, or even lead it, are not as equipped as they need to be? I'm not talking about strapping on enough information or skills; I'm talking about proven character and godliness that is woven into the heart. Do you merely distribute truth, or are your people smitten with the Truth Giver? Do your people pop up in worship like a flash mob in a shopping mall, or do they genuinely worship as a daily lifestyle?

Does your impact travel the kingdom road, from the Father to you to others and back to the Father when you give him glory in the process? This path of healthy impact is like the water cycle: rain falls, permeates the earth, and evaporates back to its source. Is your impact as refreshing, as restorative, as redemptive as *that*?

I like Barna's description of mature and equipped believers: they are "friends and imitators of Christ." One of the first topics our Life-on-Life Journey Groups address is personal worship. We teach it, model it, coach it, and participate in it together as a group. Personal worship leads to personal transformation. And God uses transformed lives to transform lives. That is where impact begins.

For too long the church has focused on numerical growth — which may well be the most accurate churchese word for success — instead of on healthy impact. The kind of church that impacts the world for the kingdom is not necessarily a growing church in terms of square footage or membership rolls. It is a healthy one. A healthy child will grow, but it isn't always true that a growing child will be healthy. In the same way, if as a church we get healthy, we'll likely grow, but just growth alone won't make us healthy. When we chose to disciple our people, we were investing in the health of our church. We understood the choice to be about obedience and impact rather than about ambition and success.

I've given healthy impact a lot of attention here because I think it is one of the primary signs of life in a church. We're many years down the road now, choosing vehicles that take us to impact rather than success, and while we don't have a perfect church, I believe we have a healthy one—in great part because of discipleship. I hesitate to use Perimeter as the only example of a healthy church. It's not. I've observed churches of all types and sizes over the years, and I have noted that, although the degree of a church's impact may vary based on the size of the church, all healthy churches—regardless of size—are also churches of impact.

Have We Lost Sight?

People often fail to realize that the endgame of spiritual development is godly character, not worldly accomplishments. God does not need his followers to achieve things on his behalf in order for them to become more acceptable or valuable to him.... Sometimes people get so wrapped up in finishing church programs or producing specific religious results that they lose sight of the purpose of their faith, which is to have a life-changing relationship with Jesus.... It becomes easy to substitute laudable religious activity for intentional and simple engagement with God. American Christians, in particular, have become known for doing good works and religious exercises rather than simply being friends and imitators of Christ.

—*George Barna, "Self-Described Christians"*

What happens when spiritual formation works? Allow me to rephrase that question: what does a healthy church look like? In the sidebar, I've listed a dozen characteristics of a healthy church, but there are three health benefits I'd like to look at more closely. We experienced them once life-on-life missional discipleship became part of our DNA. We couldn't help but notice these obvious results.

Leaders Emerged

I've already said that some of our leaders are men I led to Christ and discipled personally. They weren't all born leaders. They didn't necessarily aspire to be leaders. They *became* leaders during the process of discipleship. Life-on-life is not a program that we launched but rather a movement that we seeded. These men — and most of our women in leadership as well — grew out of discipleship. One of our elders commented recently, "Perimeter people just seem to do the right thing." I don't think he was boasting. He simply noticed that people who learn to *be* right, *do* right. This doesn't mean there aren't plenty of others out there who also do the right thing; it just means the life-on-life model has the potential to produce a critical mass of mature, equipped followers, so much so that people sit up and take notice.

Success Was Replaced by Healthy Impact

I've said plenty about this already. Paying close attention to the spiritual formation of the people in our care definitely took us down the road less traveled. It wasn't an easy, wide, or fast road. We knew it might not produce the kinds of successful results other churches enjoyed. But as redundant as this may sound, opting for healthy impact turned us into a people who would settle for nothing less than making an impact. It is a circular phenomenon. Have we experienced failure at times? You bet. Have we had success along the way? Yes, of course. But success is never the goal, which makes it icing on the cake when it occurs.

Twelve Characteristics of Healthy Churches

1. They embark on a journey of faith.
2. They choose impact over success.
3. They embrace ministries of the head, heart, and hand.
4. They are intentional about making mature and equipped followers of Christ.
5. They equip their people to appropriate the power of the Holy Spirit.
6. They emphasize the marriage of grace and duty.
7. They destroy the ministry idols of tradition and preference.
8. They don't compromise spiritual nutrition for the sake of simplicity and growth.
9. They provide healthy environments for worship and feeding rather than environments for entertainment and self-help inspiration.
10. They correctly steward the keys to the kingdom and the sacraments.
11. They underscore all their teaching with the realities of the authentic gospel and of Christ as the only hope of glory.
12. They allow their pastor to spend the time necessary for shepherding through his teaching, leading, and equipping.

And everyone knows you can't stay healthy if your diet is nothing but sugar.

The Head, the Heart, and the Hands Started Working Together

Perimeter has long been on a journey to integrate these three aspects of knowing and following Christ. For years, we did a good job leading people to feed themselves on the Word (the head) and worship God with everything in them (the heart), but we realized our commitment to justice and mercy (the hands) was underdeveloped. We weren't adequately reaching outside our four walls to those who needed not only the gospel but also food, clothing, shelter, education, advocacy, and the embrace of healthy people. Once our staff and elders chose a clear path to correct the problem, our Journey Groups got on board. These groups are where the church experiences health in the most intimate and holistic way. Not only are our leaders charged with instructing the heads and hearts of the people in their groups; they are encouraged to galvanize their hands for mission as well. Although ministry outside the four walls of the church is typically inconvenient, our Community Outreach department has made *finding* an outlet for ministry to the community easier than it used to be. They provide countless ways these groups can engage regularly in hands-on ministry to their neighbors. Of course, most churches cannot fund or staff an entire department devoted to making these connections between their people and the needs outside their four walls. That doesn't mean they can't be missional. If there are needs within a few square miles of a church — and there are if there are people and homes and schools — and if there are mission-hearted people in the church, then a few strategic relationships can build a bridge to the community.

The missional label in LOLMD is a large one. It not only refers to hands offering aid outside the walls of the church. It encompasses something far bigger than that. It marries community service to personal evangelism. In our Journey curriculum, "Mission" involves members of every group discovering ways to be on mission in their own lives, where they live, work, and play. And while mercy ministry outside the walls of the church is modeled and encouraged, evangelism is stressed as well. We cannot talk about mission in our groups without teaching and coaching people to share their faith. Mission is a holistic endeavor.

Zero to Sixty, or Getting to the Right Destination

Christians who make an impact plot the course of their lives by the coordinates of God's Word rather than the coordinates of the culture around them. David said, "Direct me in the path of your commands, for there I find delight" (Ps. 119:35). In the same way, churches that want to make an impact must make the Scriptures their primary guide. That doesn't mean we shouldn't be sensitive to the culture; it just means we must serve a Master who supersedes culture. Faithful obedience to God and his Word is the *tested* path of impact: "Your promises have been thoroughly tested" (Ps. 119:140). And the path we take determines the vehicle we use.

Imagine shipping a shiny new sports car to a coffee bean grower in southern Rwanda. Getting it there is the first challenge, not just because of the cost of shipping but also because Rwanda is landlocked with no port of entry. Even if you could fly it into Kigali International Airport, the car might not make its final destination. The very reason Rwanda is a prime spot for growing coffee beans — its altitude — is another reason a sports car might never make it from Kigali, the capital in the center of the country, to southern Maraba, the agricultural region. Don't even think about driving it down there during one of the two rainy seasons. An automobile that looks impressive on the road in the United States might look ridiculous on the dirt roads of Maraba. Forget the snappy color. The car will be coated in the mud of Africa by the first mile. Forget the zero-to-sixty acceleration. Unless you want to stall the engine ... repeatedly. Forget the "executive class amenities." Odds are the Bluetooth won't work in the jungle. You might as well keep your sports car at home in the US where it fits those roads and those destinations. For this road, buy a bike.

The sports car or the bicycle? There's nothing inherently moral or immoral about either. The fact that one looks cooler, goes faster, and makes a better impression really doesn't figure into this equation at all. Neither does the apparently sacrificial nature of the slower, less impressive, more ordinary vehicle. But once you've chosen a destination and mapped the route to get there, the choice becomes clear.

The Journey
Part Three

Donna made sure to arrive at Lisa's on time—not early—this week. When she'd heard Patricia's story over lunch the day after their last meeting, she thought of suggesting to her that she call Lisa. But she quickly dismissed the thought. That would be unfair to Lisa, who had her own share of troubles. Donna knew from experience how disheartening another mother's story could be, especially when that mother had lived it for a long, long time. Sam, Lisa's son, was still young. Sure, a rebellious middle schooler could be a challenge. For that matter, almost *every* middle schooler could be a challenge! Misery loves company and all that, but to subject the younger mom to the older mom's story, to what surely would seem like the worst-case scenario, well, how could that possibly help Lisa? Patricia's son Adam had begun rebelling in middle school too, had fathered a child with a girl who could handle neither motherhood nor giving her child up for adoption, and was now serving time in prison on drug charges. There was hope there, Donna knew it, but would Lisa be able to see it, or would Patricia's story only serve to deepen her despair over her own son? Better just to leave things alone.

This wasn't the first time Donna had underestimated a member of one of her Journey Groups and, in doing so, underestimated what God could do in their lives. A few days after their lunch date, Patricia called Donna and quietly announced, "I did something yesterday that I thought I'd regret ... but I don't."

Donna could tell she didn't need to interrupt with a "What's that?" Patricia's tone made it clear she wanted to spill her news.

"I called Lisa and asked if we could talk. We're going to meet before group next week."

"You're kidding!" Donna said. Then she added a bit less enthusiastically, "That's great."

"Well," Patricia said, "after you and I had lunch, I realized how much lighter I felt having told you the whole story. It was so cathartic, so healing. I realized I'd been in a prison of my own making because I was too ashamed to open up with anyone. I'd even pretended I was just babysitting Ethan instead of raising him because our son is in jail. My son's bad choices, while they break my heart, weren't the only thing that was killing me. It was being dishonest. When you and I talked, I finally dragged the whole mess out from under a rock and into the light. And you know what?" Patricia asked this last question almost lightheartedly.

"What?"

"You didn't judge me. You didn't judge Adam either. I know you don't know my son, but I know you love him because I do, and I know you'll pray for him. Lisa needs that ... not just from you, but from all of us."

As Donna approached Lisa's front door and raised her hand to knock, she stopped short. Through the gleaming mullioned windows, framed at the end of the foyer by the archway into the kitchen, she saw the two women sitting knee to knee, their heads bowed till they almost touched. Donna stood watching for a moment, unwilling to interrupt what was clearly a moment of prayer, until Lisa and Patricia both raised their heads and embraced each other. When Donna entered the kitchen a minute later, both women met her with the vestiges of tears on their faces. She marveled at the way tears could be transformed so quickly into beaming smiles of joy.

"Where's Ethan?" Heather, Allison, and Billie each asked Patricia when they joined the group in the kitchen minutes later.

"My husband took the morning off so I could come alone today," Patricia said with a lilt in her voice. Donna could tell each woman struggled to hide her curiosity. According to what they had observed so far, lilts weren't Patricia's style.

After going over their memory verses, Donna cleared her throat and moved to the edge of her chair. The disciplines they learned in the Journey Group were vital, but she always felt they needed to be balanced with a heavy dose of grace. Although she had stressed it before, she wanted to remind each of these women that their relationship with God wasn't founded upon the disciplines. Memorizing and studying Scripture, prayer, and worship—these were aids to that relationship, not the relationship itself. She opened her mouth to remind them yet another time.

"Donna," Patricia said, glancing over at Lisa, "Lisa and I are ready to share our journeys with the group. Do you mind if I go ahead before I lose my nerve?"

"Of course," Donna said. Her little speech about grace could wait.

"I'm a pastor's kid," Patricia began, "so you'd think I would have understood the gospel as soon as I could read. But I'm not sure I did at all. I used to say I didn't hear the gospel in my home or my church growing up, but that's not true. I just didn't hear it in my heart." She placed her palm on her chest. "I rebelled in high school. Not in ways that ... well, not anything you might consider all that bad, but my heart was far from God and I played on the edges of sin, which—I know now—is no different from diving into sin."

Patricia shared her experience of coming to Christ her senior year in high school, meeting her husband, Bob, in college, and the birth of their three children, all boys, in quick succession. Until moving from another city three years ago, they had been leaders in their church. Patricia taught women's Bible studies. As her children grew, she became the "older woman" young moms flocked to for advice. Her husband was an elder and her boys were involved heavily in their church's youth group. The two older sons, Matt and Andrew, were now married to wonderful women and living nearby. But Adam, well, Adam had rocked their world.

"I was familiar with the term 'crisis of faith,'" Patricia said, "but I had never in my life experienced one until Adam was in middle school. It started with him smoking cigarettes in the parking lot at church. Not long after that, a friend confided to us that her daughter was worried about Adam. According to her, he was smoking pot at school and drinking on the weekends. We didn't believe it. Adam was such a wild child by then, we had him on a very short leash. He had no discretionary money to spend. There was just no way. But it was all true ... and then some." Patricia shook her head ruefully.

"I won't belabor this part of my story," Patricia said, and there were some murmurs indicating that no one would object if she did. "Adam is basically an addict. His drug habit has led to so much heartache." She stopped and seemed to be thinking through her next words carefully. "Actually, his *choices* have been so hurtful. To him more than to us. Ethan was born to a young lady who couldn't take responsibility for him any more than Adam could. If ever there was a time when Bob and I knew God's will with certainty, the decision to take Ethan into our home was it. It's not what I thought we'd be doing in our empty-nest season, but how could we do anything else?

"I guess you could say Ethan is the silver lining in this story. But this week I've discovered another." She smiled at Lisa. "So until now I've not shared much about Adam with anybody. I'm a pastor's kid, remember? I'm supposed to be perfect. Our kids went through Christian school. They were in a great youth group. We had family devotions, for heaven's sake. I've not only been embarrassed; I've been bitter. How could God let this happen when we did everything right? I mean, I know I wasn't a perfect mom, but I did the best I knew how to do. And look what happened. It's like two plus two doesn't equal four."

For the first time since she'd begun her story, Patricia's eyes shone with tears. Lisa leaned over the arm of the sofa and patted Patricia on the knee. There was something so maternal in the younger woman's gesture, everyone couldn't help but smile. Donna was reminded how poignant, and yet powerful, a simple act of encouragement could be.

"So far, I've told two people. Now I've told five. And I didn't implode," she said with a crooked smile. "That's kind of amazing. But this week, when I read Paul's rebuke of the Galatians for going back to the law, I realized for the first time that I'd been relying on myself and how well I performed to please God. You'd think I'd know better by now. I guess I'm just stubborn."

Patricia took a deep breath, placed her palms on her knees, and said, "God's grace set me free. I was on day four of my Twenty-One Days of Personal Worship ... I missed day ten and had to start over."

Everyone chuckled because each one of them, with the exception of Heather, had started over at least once. "This time I took the time to really meditate on the first few verses of Galatians 5. After I finished, I knew I had to share what I'd learned, so I called Lisa. All the heartache with Adam is just so painful, but knowing God's grace and trusting him enough to open up with all of you ... well, that's wonderful."

Lisa got up from her place on the sofa and knelt next to Patricia. "Donna, I think we should stop right now and pray for Adam. Is that okay?"

Donna took a split-second inventory of their time. Patricia's journey had taken up a big chunk of their allotted time, but no one—including Donna—had dared to look at a watch or the antique regulator clock that chimed the half hour from its perch above the fireplace. There was a lot of material to cover, but it could wait. She nodded at Lisa, and the women bowed their heads to pray. Before she could tell them they didn't have to each pray out loud, Lisa began to pray for her friend. Allison prayed next, and after a stretch of silence that was only a little bit awkward, Donna ended the impromptu prayer time.

Lisa's story, while shorter and less dramatic, echoed Patricia's in many ways. She was still reeling from the choices her children were making. Until recently, she'd wondered where God was in the middle of it all. Lisa ended hopefully: "Almost every day, thanks to being *forced* to read God's Word," she said with a hint of playful sarcasm, "I am reminded that this— even this—is part of God's story. I thought the point was to do it all right and get the right results. Boy, was I missing it! This week I was reminded that I needed to experience the gospel more fully, to let Jesus' preaching and healing touch me, and then I could be a part of his mission of preaching and healing."

Donna waited a moment to be sure Lisa was finished, and then said, "Lisa, thanks for sharing. I think we can all relate to viewing life as a formula instead of a relationship. Does anyone have questions for Lisa?"

"I just have to say that your stories scare me," Heather said, looking from Lisa to Patricia, her tan face ashen. "I mean, my kids are young. I'm doing two plus two and the fact that it might not turn out to be four terrifies me! I have to be honest. I keep wondering what you did wrong."

Heather's question hung in the air for a fleeting moment while Donna tried to formulate a response, but Patricia beat her to it.

"Plenty! I did plenty wrong. Don't you think we all do? I loved my kids and taught them godly principles from the Word, but they each have a free will. They get to make their own choices and they were born with something I have too: a sin nature," Patricia said with a thin strand of sadness in her voice. "But it's not over yet. If my heavenly Father could win over *my* heart, I can trust him to win Adam's too."

"I know; it's just frightening," Heather admitted, "and right now it seems easier to keep doing the formula rather than let God do his work."

"I wouldn't stop doing what you're doing," Patricia said. "Just know the formula is a poor substitute for God's glory. Trusting him is the better part of obeying him."

"How did you get so wise?" Heather asked, effectively erasing the hurtful suggestion that Patricia had "done something wrong" as a mother.

Donna had the sensation a crisis had just been averted. Parenting is a delicate subject among mothers, especially with a mix of wounded veterans and hopeful new moms like this. Heather was abrupt, but she meant well. Donna could tell neither Patricia nor Lisa were as offended as they could have been.

Donna led the group through the material, being careful to guide the discussion without lecturing. The women grappled with the Scripture together, pausing from time to time to make sure they understood the main points. They talked at length about the verses they had studied as homework.

"Okay, ladies," Donna said, "let's do one last exercise. Turn to page nine in your Journey Guide. Did anyone list five needs of people where you live, work, or play? If so, can you share them so we can pray together? Use first names only and especially be careful if you share about your husband! Let's go around the room and each share at least one need."

Billie, who had been quiet during the meeting, brushed her bangs from her forehead and said, "Pray for my husband, David. He lost his job last week, and he's not taking it very well. I had the audacity to tell him I was praying for him," she said with a grin, "and he just laughed at me. Well, I told him he'd better watch out 'cause God answers prayer! So I need you to get out your big guns and pray."

Billie's confidence was at once exhilarating and disconcerting. Later, when Donna prayed for her privately at home, she asked God to answer Billie's naive prayer and to use her childlike faith to get her husband's attention and not to give him reason to mock her further.

Heather asked for prayer for two women on her tennis team. Lisa asked for prayer for her mother-in-law, a negative woman made more so these days because of chronic pain. Allison had three friends in a weekly neighborhood play group who did not know Jesus. She asked for courage to share her faith with them.

"Allison, I don't doubt that you are fully equipped to share with them," Donna said, "but if you'd like to invite them out for coffee or lunch with me, I'd be happy to talk with them. You could say your 'life coach' or 'mentor' has been helpful to you and you just want them to benefit too. What do you think?"

Allison looked relieved. "I'd love that," she said. "I'll let you know how they respond. One of them—Callie—would jump at the chance. I can tell she's spiritually hungry."

"I know this sounds bad," Patricia said, "but I have been so focused on my immediate family lately, I had a hard time with this question. Pray that I would widen my view. The only name I wrote down was Pam. She and her kids have so many needs, so that's who I'd like us to pray for today."

"Who's Pam?" Billie asked.

"Our mail lady," Patricia said with a grin, adding, "I don't get out much."

"Actually," Donna admitted, "our mail lady is on my list too. I've known her for sixteen years, as long as we've lived in our house. Her name is Betty. I know the gospel can apply to her life through my words and deeds, I'm just not sure how. So I need you to pray for her with me."

Once again, heads were bowed and prayers were lifted, and a suburban living room became a "house of prayer."

What's in a Name?

What It Means to Disciple

Shakespeare said a rose by any other name would smell as sweet, but I'm not so sure about that.

The names of things matter, if not as much as their meanings. On the other hand, I'm pretty certain the church today has paid a little too much attention to branding. What started as an attempt to communicate more relevantly has evolved, in some cases, into market strategies as obsessive, as costly, and as pervasive in church culture as any ad campaign cranked out of Madison Avenue. In the process, the name of the rose has become more important than the rose itself. So which is it? Do we define the things that matter, or do we just hope the labels we affix to them give them definition?

I think you know how I would answer that question. We have never been content with a general yet compelling description of discipleship. We had to be sure exactly what we were going to do, to define it first.

All by itself, there's a lot packed into the phrase we finally came up with: life-on-life missional discipleship. We expanded that phrase into a paragraph: "Life-on-life missional discipleship is laboring in the lives of a few with the intention of imparting one's life, the gospel, and God's Word in such a way as to see them become mature and equipped followers of Christ, committed to doing the same in the lives of others."

The definition evolved in the doing, and along the way, we named it. The name is important because it marks the history of this evolution, and it matches the process of discipleship as we know it today. In a moment, I will work backward, giving a more complete definition of life-on-life missional discipleship. But first, I want to place such discipleship in the broader context of the church's ministry. The picture looks something like figure 3.

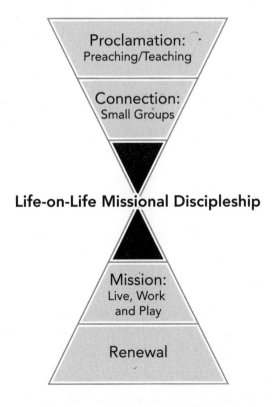

Figure 3

Two challenges in any discussion about discipleship involve its definition and its degrees. I've already discussed the definition of discipleship. The concept of the degrees of discipleship can be explained with an hourglass diagram.

At the top of the hourglass is proclamational discipleship, which comes through preaching and teaching. Some believe that if you just faithfully proclaim the gospel, then people will become mature and missional believers. No doubt, God uses the proclamation of his Word to justify the sinner and sanctify the saint. But proclamational discipleship alone is not sufficient to make mature and equipped followers of Christ.

Many churches have used various types of small groups as part of their discipleship strategy (home groups, life groups, fellowship groups, community groups, etc.). Many pastors acknowledge that these types of small groups provide community but are not sufficient to make mature and equipped followers of Christ. These groups often have a missional expectation, but I've observed that mission doesn't happen as much as was hoped for. Excellent small groups have elements of both proclamation and incarnation.

However, the missing piece of the discipleship hourglass is the middle section called Life-on-Life Missional Discipleship. These groups combine a mission and a nurture component, which is why growth seems to happen at an accelerated pace. When there is a missional bias in these types of groups, you get nurture thrown in. If you focus only on nurture, you may or may not get mission. Since the church is a home, a mission, and an equipping station, all these degrees of discipleship form a strong strategy for making mature and equipped followers of Christ.

In light of this, let's now unpack our label "life-on-life missional discipleship" word by word.

Discipleship

We acknowledge that we've co-opted a word that is centuries old and quite general in meaning and narrowed it to fit deeper applications. But that doesn't mean our definition of discipleship isn't *biblical*; we are convinced that it is. Looking at some of the other words that refer to "disciples" in the New Testament helps to give us a sense of just how weighty this word — *discipleship* — really is. In the book of Acts, Luke uses a variety of different names to describe followers of Christ. Because Acts is a book of descriptions, not prescriptions, we can get a fairly clear sense of what it meant to be a disciple in the first century. Luke wrote *about* the first Christians, unlike Paul, who wrote *to* them.

The Greek root word for *disciple* used most often in the New Testament is *mathetes*. Luke uses this word thirty times in Acts alone. The word in all its forms refers to a learner, an adherent, or an apprentice. It was first used in Greek literature about five hundred years before Christ by Herodotus, and later by Socrates, Pythagoras, and others. Although it still presumed an academic context, the word eventually came to mean a learner's personal, life commitment to a prominent teacher or master.[8]

Those who followed Jesus would have understood the term *mathetes* right away. Disciples of Jesus would have been distinguished from other people by the simple fact that their master and teacher was Jesus. And what a master he was! By the time the book of Acts was written, those who called themselves disciples of Jesus had the distinction of following a teacher who had been crucified, had risen from the dead, and had left behind his Holy Spirit to teach and lead his students.

Another word in the book of Acts fleshes out the meaning of discipleship in the first century. In Acts 2:44 and Acts 10:45, the word *believer* (*ho pisteuontes* and *hoi pistoi*, respectively) is used, both times in reference to new believers who were being added to the church. Referring to a disciple as a "believer" reminds us that a disciple is anyone who chooses to trust in Jesus for salvation and for all of life.

Several words and phrases in Acts also describe the kind of lives believers lived and the kind of people they were. In at least one instance, believers are referred to as those "who belonged to the Way" (9:2), and we read in Acts 11:26 that for the first time in history, followers of Jesus are called Christians (from the Greek

Cristianou, which literally means "Christ men"). Here, and in the other instances where this term is used in Scripture (see 1 Peter 4:16), the earliest followers of Jesus did not use the label *Christian* to describe themselves. The early disciples likely would have considered it somewhat presumptuous to use their Savior's name this way. Instead, *Christian* was a term used by an unbelieving Gentile world to show scorn and disdain for people who would identify their lives so closely with a crucified Jewish rabbi.

When Jesus' followers referred to one another, they spoke of their relationships in a familiar way, referring to other Christ followers as brother or sister. In Acts 1:15 – 16, Luke records that Peter addressed his brothers (*adelphoi*) and sisters (*adelphe*). Disciples of Jesus in the first century understood that they weren't just classmates listening to the same teacher; they were united by bonds stronger than the desire to learn; they were now a family.

In addition to describing the disciples as being *learners* sitting at the foot of their teacher, *believers* trusting their master to lead them, *followers* of the Way, *Christians* who look like smaller versions of Christ, and *brothers* and *sisters* in their relationship to one another, Luke adds one more word to describe the disciples. In at least four verses, he refers to the early disciples as *hoi hagioi*, or saints. The term *saint* comes from a root word that speaks of awe and reverence offered to God alone. *Saint* is a word that elevates the meaning of disciple from a pupil in a classroom to someone who is bound in love and worship to the God of the universe. A true disciple is someone who, once he or she is born into the family, can never go back to the orphanage, whose earthly DNA is exchanged for heavenly DNA.

As you can see, the words *disciple* and *discipleship* are both used broadly in our context. For that reason, we add a few more descriptive words to bring clarity.

Missional

"Who do you think is the greatest pastor the United States has ever known?"

I ask pastors and leaders this question on occasion, and I almost always hear the same answer: Jonathan Edwards. Edwards pastored what I call a "three-strand church" — a church that includes three elements in balance with one another. First, his ministry addressed the "heads" of those in his care, with a goal of sound doctrine. Second, Edwards addressed the "heart." Not content to fill the mind, he called for passion in worship and in the proclamation of the gospel. He understood that to encounter God in worship is an experience that goes beyond reasoning about truth: "It must be a more immediate, sensible discovery that must give the mind a real sense of the excellency and beauty of God."[9] Finally, Jonathan Edwards addressed the "hand," leading his church to do acts of mercy and justice. Members of the church lived out in their communities the realities they affirmed in their heads and hearts.

These three strands are rarely found together in today's churches. Most churches tend to emphasize one strand, often at the expense of the other two. Heads-only churches all too easily devolve into dead orthodoxy. Hearts-only churches can major on emotionalism without adequate declaration of truth. And hands-only churches may succumb to a bland liberalism that offers bread without offering the Bread of Life.

As I compared Perimeter with the balance promoted by Edwards, I realized that at best, we were just a two-strand church. We were doing a more than decent job challenging heads and hearts, but we were not mobilizing hands well. Chip Sweney, a member of our staff who was working with our junior high students at the time we were thinking about all of this, explains it this way:

> In 2001, [Randy] explained a simple paradigm of a healthy church:
>
> **head (theology) + heart (passion) + hand (external ministry)**
>
> Randy shared with the Perimeter staff that he felt the church was missing this last key ingredient, the hand. He confessed his regret that our church was not strategically caring

for those with significant needs outside of our own doors. As Perimeter neared the celebration of its twenty-fifth anniversary, he charged the leaders to devise a plan to engage with the community and serve its needs.[10]

Chip alludes to the fact that, while we were shepherding our own people well, we had neglected the people who lived outside our own four walls—not completely, but significantly. So in 2001, we began a major shift toward becoming an influential church. Chip eventually became the head of our Community Outreach ministry, an arm of the church that helps connect the people inside the church with the many ministry opportunities outside Perimeter. Chip helped birth and now leads the movement we call Unite!, the fusing in relationship and purpose of more than one hundred and twenty churches in our area to transform our community with the practical love of Christ.

This missional shift wasn't something we just tacked onto our programming. It was woven into the life of our church at all levels. Though at the time we were already engaging in life-on-life discipleship, we added another adjective to fill out what we were doing: the word *missional*. Our discipleship needed the balance of the head, the heart, *and* the hand. This shift in our life-on-life discipleship emphasis was more than just semantics. It tipped the scales of our discipleship, changing our curriculum for discipleship training in such a way that our practices are now heavily weighted with sections that help individual believers discern God's purpose for their lives and develop within themselves a biblical worldview. The "work" of discipleship is not just informational, nor is it simply relational; it must be action oriented as well. And that means propelling disciples outward, to the community around us, to engage in acts of mercy and justice.

As I have mentioned, mission is more than just mercy ministry, but it is certainly not less. In our Journey Groups, we stress the importance of individuals getting into the world of others. We talk about how mission is more than a church program; it is part of our call to follow Jesus, something that must be reflected in the life of every believer. That's why we talk so much in our groups about the need to be on mission where people live, work, and play. As group members become involved in the lives of their neighbors, their coworkers, and their unbelieving friends, they are encouraged not only to meet needs but to address the greatest need any of us has, our need to know Jesus and place our trust in him. We have come to understand that to be a church of healthy impact, we must begin to see our mission more broadly: proclaiming the mercy of God as expressed in the gospel to a lost world and demonstrating the fruit of that mercy to a world in need of healing and hope.

To give you an idea of how systemic this change has been, I've asked Chip to tell you just a bit more of his story:

> As a leader and staff member at Perimeter, I was required to do more than promote programs; I was to share my life in discipleship relationships. We were all accountable to operate on this basic level, including Randy. Jesus did it. His disciples did it. And they passed the pattern along to the next generation.
>
> When members of a church are engaged in life-on-life missional discipleship, the church is the healthiest it can be, the most holistic. It is a church where heads, hearts, and hands join together. For example, before Randy's vision eventually grew to become a fully staffed Community Outreach department, I was meeting regularly for discipleship with a group of junior high boys. At the same time, I was prompted by the Spirit to lead in the area of ministry to the community. It just made sense — at this basic, cellular level — to involve my teenage guys in mission. We studied the Word together, we shared our lives, and we began meeting once a month to tutor children in need. All three elements in concert made the picture complete.
>
> When discipleship is going on in a church, it's hard to compartmentalize its ministries. Missions becomes more than a program of the church — it becomes the natural response of people in relationships responding to God's call. Giving becomes a communal act borne out of more than a sermon on tithing. Worship is a dance of interwoven lives in motion. Holiness is organic and real, something each person hammers out in the

context of discussion and debate and the support of friends. And a movement — like the gathering firestorm of Unite! — can be as deep as it is wide.[11]

Life-on-Life

When I speak to pastors and leaders, I often ask them to do a simple exercise. I have them write down their church's top five offerings to help their people in spiritual formation. After they turn in their answers, I define spiritual formation for them by describing a mature and equipped follower of Christ. I ask them to look at their five offerings and then pose the question, "Do all of your offerings get people to the destination I've just described? If so, raise your hand." Often there will be no hands raised. How discouraging! Invariably, the collective list is skewed toward up-front events designed to dispense truth in scattershot fashion, events that get warm bodies in pews or big programs that generate all kinds of activity and involvement. Sometimes these are the only items on the list. And again, let me be clear: it's not that these events and programs don't help people in spiritual formation; they do. But they fail to take people to the destination, and they don't adequately equip them for the journey. There is an obvious disconnect between what the church offers and what people really need.

When leaders think about discipleship, the image that comes up, consciously or not, is not an hourglass; it is a funnel. The idea goes something like this: "The church is a funnel where we pack as many people as we can into our buildings, our stadium seats, our programs. The more we do our events and programs with relevance and excellence, the bigger the wide end of the funnel needs to be. We have a big mission, after all, so shouldn't we go after that mission in a big context?"

"But what about the coaching and supporting part of discipleship?" I have to ask in this hypothetical conversation.

"That's where the truly committed trickle down into the narrow end of the funnel. To be honest, discipleship in a life-on-life manner is an afterthought or an addendum. At best, it's an exclusive club for the spiritually mature."

Now I'm not opposed to big-funnel church. Perimeter is a big church with big events and big programming. If growing in attendance was our primary goal, I'd be only about stretching the wide end of the funnel to the breaking point. But here is the catch: the kingdom doesn't work that way. The primary objective of a funnel is to collect as many people as we can, and that's not growth.

Instead, kingdom growth starts with something small like a seed, a tiny package in which all of the characteristics of the larger, fully grown plant dwell. When we grasp that kingdom growth reflects the type of growth we see in a seed, we recognize that we need to invert the funnel. The drama that sets the stage for lasting growth isn't what we see on the stage or in the gym where hundreds have gathered; it's in the living rooms of the houses in the suburbs, in apartment clubhouses, around kitchen tables in the projects, and in the boardrooms of city center office buildings. The motivation that propels the masses out into the world and leads to lasting spiritual growth isn't a pep rally; it's a huddle. As we were developing the process for life-on-life discipleship, we had seed-to-plant growth in mind. We understood that to effectively produce disciples, we needed to invert the funnel.

Just as you'd expect, there are challenges to doing discipleship in a life-on-life manner in a large church context. I'm the first

Organic

Again [Jesus] said, "What shall we say the kingdom of God is like, or what parable shall we use to describe it? It is like a mustard seed, which is the smallest seed you plant in the ground. Yet when planted, it grows and becomes the largest of all garden plants, with such big branches that the birds of the air can perch in its shade."

—Mark 4:30–32

to admit that this is hard. It's a lot easier just to herd everyone into a big room and preach. And there are practical obstacles as well, obstacles that show up as soon as a potential disciple leaves college: spouses, kids, jobs, schedules, traffic, homes, yards, vacations. I'll address these issues in later chapters, but for now it's important to acknowledge that they exist. And because they do, it's imperative to approach spiritual formation on a seedling level. You'll give up if you are not convinced it's the best way. An entry in my journal from 1999, once LOLMD had gained traction among our staff, reflects how convinced I was:

Journal—8/4/99

I spent the whole of yesterday meeting with our staff. All went well. We certainly have an outstanding group of servant-leaders. We asked each staff to share their status regarding involvement in discipleship this coming September. Over 90 percent (probably high 90s), including support staff, are either leading a group or in a group. It's now being modeled from the top down. My hope for the future effectiveness of our church is bound in discipleship. I long to see church growth taking place by multiplication (in decentralized groups) as opposed to by addition (in the centralized weekly gathering).

I feel like I'm leading a grand experiment which, though biblically based, has unusually high stakes. To fail will more than likely deflate my zeal and hope for giving my life in the leadership of an American church. But I remain convinced that we will accomplish the task. We may first have to become fewer and tighter as a church to get my arms around the team of players that will make it happen. It is my job to plant and water, but God's to cause the growth. I must remain fixed on running the race with the proper motives rather than consumed with concern regarding the results of the marathon.

Lord, thanks for allowing me to run for your glory. May every stride be fully devoted to you. I love you.

One reason "fewer and tighter" is a discipleship nonnegotiable—and every bit worth the risk—is that the narrow end of the funnel is where authenticity can thrive. To take a picture of a large group, a photographer must step back and use a wide-angle lens. The bigger the group, the fuzzier the result. No one looks all that bad in a group picture, but you don't really notice anyone either. But to take a portrait, the focus is sharper and the perspective is up close, revealing flaws that weren't visible in the group shot. Life-on-life is spiritual formation with a telescopic lens; it brings life up close and personal so that no one can hide or, worse, fall through the cracks. For that reason it can be messy and, well, *real*.

My wife, Carol, has experienced this kind of authenticity in her relationships with the women she has led in groups over the years. Not long ago, one of the women in her current group sent an email to her group that champions the beauty of life-on-life better than anything else I could say about it:

> Just wanted to write a few thoughts about how blessed we are to be in a group of authentic women. I was thinking through my own journey over the last years and wanted to thank each of you because:
>
> > You loved me when I felt unlovable.
> > You gave me value when I felt worthless.
> > You embraced me when I felt condemned.
> > You didn't think less of me when I felt judged.
> > You encouraged me when I felt scorned by the world.
> > You cared for me when I wanted to self-destruct.
> > You held me up when I wanted to fall.
> > You told me the truth when I wanted to listen to lies.
> > You were strong when I was weak.
> > You showed me how to breathe when life took my breath away.
> > You were Jesus when I needed him in flesh and bone.
> > You understood, even though your flesh could not.
> > You called me when I felt I had nothing to say.
> > You made me face the day when I wanted to tread in darkness.
> > You challenged me when I wanted to be mindless.

You loved my family when others found them unlovable.
You asked me questions when I just wanted to blend in.
You saw God's potential in me when I saw nothing.
You knew me when I didn't recognize myself.

Relational discipleship, so much more than Bible study.
Thanks for "doing life" with me![12]

One other reason discipleship occurs most effectively at the seedling, life-on-life level is that when growth happens in this real, transparent, deep way, that way of growth itself is reproduced. Seeds produce more than plants. They manufacture, in the heart of the new plants, more seeds. And thus the small end of the funnel explodes into a wider context. A blade of grass becomes a lush lawn. A sprout of heirloom wheat becomes a meadow filled with grain. An acorn becomes a stand of majestic oaks. And the story goes on and on, uncontained and unstoppable, covering the earth with the glory of God.

The Journey
Men's Journey Group

To give you a well-rounded perspective, I've included one glimpse here into a men's Journey Group. For obvious reasons, I know a lot more about what goes on in this particular variety of discipleship. Although this vignette, like the ladies', is fictional, I hope you'll see that the interaction between men, while quite different from the women, is open and at times even vulnerable. That's one reason LOLMD is such a powerful agent for change in men's lives.

"I can't emphasize this point enough," Donna's husband, Hank, said to the group of men gathered around the conference table in Tom Hanna's office. The fluorescent light above them flickered for just a moment as dawn began its slow appearance through the tall bank of windows on one side of the room. The men met every week at 6:00 a.m., usually leaving before the receptionist arrived and unlocked the office for the day.

"This is all about developing a love relationship," Hank reminded them, "not measuring performance."

He looked around the room and wondered if these guys

got it yet. A few of the men were real movers and shakers. The kind of guys who loved a challenge. They measured everything, and more often than not they came out on top. Mark was of the overachiever breed. But there were times when Hank wondered what was behind his sterling track record. He knew there was more to this sharp young man, and he hoped Mark eventually would open up about his struggles. On the other hand, Hank was pretty sure he saw relief in the eyes of the two men who had lost their jobs recently. Another was still reeling from an unwanted divorce. These men were well aware that they needed God's grace.

After going over their memory verses, with the reminder that the purpose of memorization was meditation, Hank introduced the morning's meeting with a question.

"We've been learning about God's glory. As you have studied and thought about it, has this idea of glory made any difference in your life?"

After a short pause, Tom said, "You know, it has helped me identify counterfeit glories."

"What do you mean, specifically?" Hank asked.

"Well, first I can see it when others pursue them. I mean, just watch ESPN for fifteen minutes, and there's a story of an athlete who has made his physical prowess his god. Now, even though I admire a player's talent, I see how unsatisfying it is to worship that kind of acclaim."

Tom shook his head and went on. "But that's not all. It's so easy to think I have to be the last one to leave the office or the first one to volunteer for a project that will take me away from home for days at a time. Nothing's wrong with working hard, but I'm beginning to see that God's glory is healthier than man's glory. I've shortchanged my wife and kids too many times because I was seeking counterfeit glory in my career."

"That's a hard one to admit, Tom," Hank said. "Thanks for sharing."

The men nodded, and a few murmured their agreement.

"Let's move on to the Truth and Equipping section of the

Journey Guide," Hank said, sensing that the men, while they appreciated Tom's comments, were glad to move away from a topic that was awkward for some. They would have to revisit that one, he thought.

"I'm going to draw the entire chart found on page five," Hank explained as he pulled out a blank sheet of paper and placed it where everyone could see.

He illustrated the two ways of gaining God's favor, by performance or by grace, and then explained that performance is based on what we *do*, on our self-righteousness, and that grace is based on what God has already *done*, on his righteousness deposited within us through Christ.

For the sake of Jim, an older man who had only recently come to Christ and who had no church background whatsoever, Hank talked at length about the demonstrative righteousness described in the book of James and the declarative righteousness described in Paul's letters.

"So, wait a minute," Jim said. "You said our righteousness is all about what God has done, not what we do. Where does this demonstrative righteousness fit in? I'm not sure I get it."

"Anyone want to take a stab at this?" Hank asked.

"Well," Brad Simpson said, "I think it means we actually do righteous things, but only as a result of what Christ has done in us ... or something like that."

"That's right," Hank said. "Good job making it clearer. I'd say our demonstrations of righteousness also flow from gratitude for what God has already done for us. Does that make sense, Jim?"

"Yeah, it does. Thanks, guys."

"Let's move on and take some time for personal worship," Hank said. "And again, the goal is not to make it to twenty-one days. The goal is to develop a habit of spending intimate time alone with God. Let's go over the left side of the page only and make some observations about this short passage: Colossians 1:9–10."

As the men pulled out their sheets of paper and opened

their Bibles, Hank said, "Take a few minutes and write down your observations. Just a phrase or two for each question."

After the men had finished writing, Hank said, "I'm going to share my own observations, but first, would one or two of you share yours?"

"Bottom line: I need to pray for people," said Brad.

"Okay, that's great," Hank said. "Anyone want to add to that?"

Mark cleared his throat and, to Hank's keen eye, seemed shaken. "This is pretty heavy stuff," he said. "Sometimes I wonder what I signed on for when I became a Christian as a kid. I mean, 'walking in a manner *worthy* of the Lord'? That's a tall order. I guess it's a process, right? I'm just not sure I'm as far along as I thought I was."

Hank could tell that a few of the men, the ones who knew Mark well, were surprised by his candor. And yet, this is what he had prayed and hoped for. He uttered a quick mental prayer, asking the Lord to direct him to respond in a way that would encourage, and then he said, "Mark, I think we can all relate. That's why we're here, so we can learn more about the process and actually enter into it."

"I understand," Tom broke in. "I'm not aware of any big sin in my life right now, but I struggle with mediocrity."

"What do you mean?" Hank asked.

"Well, I just don't see any dramatic growth. Even when I make my best efforts."

"Let me ask you a question, then, Tom," Hank said, "just to be sure. You aren't talking about being faithless or disobedient, right?"

"Right."

"And even when you give it your all, the results seem mediocre."

"Yeah, that can't be right, can it?"

"I hope what I'm going to say will encourage you," Hank said. "I'm not so sure God is disappointed in you about this. He doesn't look at results; he looks at the heart. Maybe this is just one of those times when the results are less than you desire, but God is pleased with you, and in my book that's what really matters."

"I don't know," Tom said. "This is a new way of looking at things, but I think you're right."

The group then spent a few minutes discussing the kingdom, that it is the reign of God, our King, over us, his subjects. Hank encouraged them to pray for more people to enter the kingdom of God. Next, he directed their attention to the Mission segment of the Journey Guide. "What do you think it means to be 'motivated by the gospel'?" he asked.

"To take up Jesus' mission?" Tom said.

"To do what he did, to seek and save the lost."

"To do that because we're so grateful for our own salvation."

"These are all great answers," Hank said. "Now let me ask you, how did Jesus seek and save the lost? Do you remember?"

"By preaching and healing."

"That's right," Hank said. "Remember, healing can mean a lot more than just physical healing. It can mean finding the need in another and meeting that need. It can also mean praying for healing for others. Any kind of healing. I encourage you to ask people if you can pray for them. I've seen non-Christians be blown away when I asked them if I could pray for them, and then, right then, I pray. More than once, I've asked a waiter if I could pray for anything specific for him. It's amazing the responses I've gotten. Sometimes that very day the person had cried out to God for help."

"That's crazy," Jim said with a low whistle. "I'm not sure I could do that."

"That's okay, Jim," Hank reassured him, "but you can pray *for* others whether you pray *with* them or not. In fact, right now I'd like for you to each list at least five people for whom you want to pray for healing of some kind."

As the men made their lists, some listing only three and

others having to stop at five or six, Hank said, "If you'd like to go out to lunch with me and anyone on your list, let's do it. I'd be happy to model sharing Christ for you, if an appropriate opportunity arises.

"Now let's end with prayer," Hank said, glancing at his watch and deciding there was time for this last exercise. "Open your Bibles to Psalm 84:10–12. As we read these three short verses, let's focus our prayer time on honor. I'll read the verses, and you can respond with a short phrase directed to God, honoring him.

"Verse 10: 'Better is one day in your courts than a thousand elsewhere; I would rather be a doorkeeper in the house of my God than dwell in the tents of the wicked.' "

"Lord, I thank you that being with you is more satisfying than being anywhere else," Tom said.

"Verse 11: 'For the LORD God is a sun and shield; the LORD bestows favor and honor; no good thing does he withhold from those whose walk is blameless.' "

Brad said, "Lord, I thank you that you share your honor with us, even though we don't deserve it."

"Verse 12: 'O LORD Almighty, blessed is the man who trusts in you.' "

And Hank ended with, "Lord, thank you that you are Lord over all and that trusting you brings blessing to our lives."

As soon as they finished praying, Tom left quickly for his office down the hall, and the others made their way to the parking lot. That Mark lingered and wanted a word with Hank was obvious.

"Hank, can we meet sometime in the next few weeks?" he said, not looking Hank in the eye.

"Sure, Mark, I'd like that."

"I'll have my assistant call you."

"You sure you don't want to talk now?" Hank asked, sensing that this was more urgent than Mark was willing to admit. "I have time."

"No, I've gotta run. But soon, okay?"

"Soon as you want," Hank said, patting Mark on the back.

Mark looked up briefly and said, "I'm slipping and I think I may need help."

He turned quickly before Hank could respond and walked away. Hank watched as he made his way down the hall, a little slumped for a step or two before he lapsed back into his normal jaunty gait, as if readying himself to meet the day. He understood that Mark's admission was a huge risk for a man who seemed to have the world on a string. "Lord, work in that young man's life," Hank prayed, "and make him ready to fall into your arms before he falls into something much, much harder."

CHAPTER SEVEN

The Tortoise and the Negative Split

Getting Started

How you begin determines everything else. And everything else figures heavily into the decisions you make about how you begin.

I know, circular reasoning, right?

This is somewhat like a track. I like to exercise, but my hour on the treadmill is nothing compared with the preparation and effort exerted by a world-class sprinter as he propels himself out of the starting blocks in the 400-meter sprint. It doesn't require a lot of thought for me to put one foot in front of the other, but for a runner who competes at the highest level, the placement of every step is a science. Especially the first one.

I've watched track-and-field events during the Olympics. I'm sure you have too. When the announcer says, "On your marks," the sprinters bend over in an intense state of readiness. When he adds, "Set," they crouch up and forward as if to say, "You thought

I was ready to run a second ago, but look at me now." And when the starter's gun fires, the runners burst from the blocks like match-lit bottle rockets or cougars pouncing on their prey. A runner's starting technique is important to his or her overall performance in the race. To give you an idea how much thought has gone into the science of the starting block, see if you can make sense of this formula:

Impulse = F × t

Maybe this will clarify things:

F = ma ... m = mass ... a = average acceleration
However, a = (vf−vi)/t ... vf = final velocity ... vi = initial velocity
Therefore, F = m(vf−vi)/t
Or, F = (mvf−mvi)/t
Hence, Ft = mvf−mvi[13]

No? It didn't help me much either. All that these equations tell me, bottom line, is that the first movement a runner makes in the very first nanosecond could very well determine the results of the race. Those who study the biomechanics of sprinting know how to fine-tune elements like the mass of a runner—his or her position in the blocks, including the hands, shoulders, and various parts of the feet—so that the maximum force is "produced for the longest practicable time. Therefore it facilitates the athlete in producing the greatest impulse and leaving the blocks with the highest velocity."[14]

Now, if discipleship were a sprint, this might have been inspirational years ago when we were just getting started, taking our first steps. All of our focus would have been on generating the maximum force and velocity, because that's what is needed to speed around a track when you run a single lap. Our discipleship likely would have rolled out like any other event or program, and we would have poured our energy into marketing for the masses, because that's what you need to ignite the big bang and get things started. But discipleship—life-on-life missional discipleship—doesn't work that way. It's not a sprint, and starting our discipleship process as if we were preparing for a sprint would have been a huge mistake.

But unfortunately, that's exactly how we did it.

Slow and Steady

Robert Chapman, the director of the Human Performance Laboratory in Indiana University's School of Health, has invested his life in learning how to best train an entirely different kind of runner: the marathoner. As you can imagine, the science involved in starting out a marathon-length run is completely different from the science of sprinting. According to Chapman, who has coached several runners for the Olympic marathon trials, the best way to start a marathon is exactly opposite to that of a sprint. You start a marathon slowly. It makes sense, doesn't it? After all, if you are going to run 26.2 miles, you can't give it

What Aesop Knew

Aesop may have recorded the tale, but the fable about the hare and the tortoise has been told, in one form or another, in many cultures — French, Swiss, German, African, Native American, and Brazilian, to name only a few. In every instance but one, the slower animal wins, and the moral is always one that denigrates haste and praises thoughtful plodding. In 1738, Sir Roger L'Estrange wrote, "A plodding Diligence brings us sooner to our Journey's End, than a fluttering Way of advancing by Starts and by Stops." A century later, Samuel Croxall wrote, in what sounds to me like a backhanded compliment to those who emulate the tortoise, that "men of dull parts, and slow apprehension, assisted by a continued diligence, are more likely to attain this, than your brisk retailers of wit."

all you've got in the first mile. You won't have anything left to complete the race. Chapman cites the "fast beginning" as one of the top four rookie mistakes first-time marathoners make.[15] He says a conservative "negative split" approach, where the first half of the race is slower so that the second half can be faster, is the only way to succeed. He cautions runners to avoid responding to all the hype at the beginning of a race — the bands, cheering crowds, even fireworks — and attempt to set a slower pace. If ever there were a champion for the tortoise, Robert Chapman is it.

As I've indicated, the process of discipleship is more like a marathon than a sprint. In our experience at Perimeter, the impact of our discipleship has broadened and deepened over time, and it continues to affect the character and quality of fellowship in our church. (I use the term *fellowship* to define those engaged in the process of life-on-life discipleship who, as a result, experience the work of God in and through their lives.) It has propelled our people to move beyond themselves into our community. But what happened in those first years? What did we do right, and what mistakes did we make in the first half of our race?

Our "negative split" in the first half of the marathon was probably not as slow as it should have been, to be honest. In our eagerness to begin maturing and equipping our people, we made two key mistakes. First, we enlisted as many people as we could, around a few hundred who populated many groups. To lead that many groups, we pressed people into service who weren't ready to lead. If they were willing to lead, we recruited them. Many lacked the skills to lead, or they didn't understand or embrace our vision of discipleship. We also failed to adequately equip the leaders we recruited. If I had everything to do over again, I would have encouraged us to begin our discipleship efforts in much the same way a business launches a new product. A beta group would test it. On the basis of that first group's experience, we would do some debugging. When the "product" is finally deemed ready, we would launch it to a broad spectrum of consumers. All of this takes time and patience, but there is great wisdom in that approach.

To put it simply, if you want to seed discipleship into the soil of your church, all you need is one group. That's what we recommend to churches today. Looking back, I'd optimistically say that 20 percent of our first groups were strong. Their leaders were equipped and mature and highly motivated to lead the people in their groups. Even if I had only one group like this, I'd begin with this group, rather than go for the big launch to the masses with immature leaders.

If our experience isn't enough to convince you, here is an observation we've made based on our work with other churches: when a church begins to implement LOLMD and they attempt too much too soon, we find that they *almost never* sustain a discipleship movement, regardless of how impressive their first year starts out. Those who begin slowly and grow steadily over years, however, tend to experience long-term shifts in the culture of their church. Beginning slow and small can actually be a positive for busy pastors as well. You don't need a large crowd, an inflated budget, or an expensive outlay of manpower to begin life-on-life missional discipleship. All it takes is one mature leader and a few committed followers.

Casting the Vision

Let's imagine that when it comes to the priority of discipleship, your church boasts only a small parade of folks who are following the tune of one lone Pied Piper playing the discipleship song. Maybe that's you and a handful of others. How does that parade become a grand procession of mature, equipped believers? To any leader the obvious answer is vision. Planning to run a race? You first have to envision the finish line. Perhaps as you look at your congregation, you see hundreds of potential marathon runners out there. But they haven't even signed up for the race yet. You have to start with the few who are willing to gather at the starting line and run toward the finish, one step at a time.

Our experience has taught us that the seed of successful discipleship is not a critical mass of people, nor is it expensive banners strategically placed in your church or a great sermon on the subject. The seed is the group itself. And this is where the vision casting must begin.

Do you remember the introduction of "New Coke" in 1985? That famous debacle led to the rebranding of the original Coke as "Coke Classic" and to the eventual demise of the new product not too many years after its launch. In an uncharacteristically awkward move, Coca-Cola cast a vision the public was not ready to receive. Too late, they discovered the "bugs" in their new product: it didn't taste good enough to pry soda-drinkers' fingers off of their traditional favorite. If your first group—and the first few groups after that—constitute the debugging stage of discipleship, common sense dictates that broad, wholesale vision casting during this phase would be a mistake. It's best not to promise what we're not certain we can deliver. It's best not to dream out loud until there is some indication that the dream will materialize.

Once discipleship has taken root, the first group has birthed other groups, the leaders are trained and ready, and—the best marketing tool around—people are buzzing about the groups, *then* it's time to take the vision public. We suggest several ways to do this. The most obvious is the pulpit. From time to time, I will preach about discipleship. Even more often, however, I will use stories from my own group as sermon illustrations (with permission, of course). Weeks prior to recruiting new groups, we host an orientation for anyone who is interested in LOLMD. At this orientation, we tell stories, give biblical support for discipleship, and set the bar high for what is required for those who decide to join a group. Most years, our church also holds a vision awareness meeting in which we lay out the vision for the coming year. Every year we include LOLMD in some form during this meeting. Again, if the seed had not produced a healthy crop, all this vision casting would be nothing more than admiration of the emperor's nonexistent new clothes. Our vision *must* reflect substance; otherwise it is nothing more than a hallucination.

Coaching

The mistakes we made when we first launched were not without consequences. We had to debug in midstride, after we had inspired the congregation with our great vision. At this point we couldn't simply disband all of our groups and start over. So we focused instead on equipping our leaders as thoroughly as we could.

Yet again, we had to learn to slow down. We wanted to do our equipping fast and big, but what our leaders needed was the small and slow. Quick efforts to train and equip people are usually a reaction to a problem, while slow and deliberate discipling naturally leads to grassroots strategizing. Big may raise up raving fans, but it also stirs up vocal detractors and everything in between. Small efforts plant deep seeds that can eventually mature into healthy dedication. Big and fast leads to a small group on steroids, a Bible study with a lot of passion but very little real growth. Small and slow is the path to life-on-life missional discipleship. This is why we have developed a wide array of coaching opportunities for our leaders. None of this was developed overnight, and I am keenly aware that not every church or leader has the ability to produce comprehensive leadership resources to train and equip people. You may have to look outside your own church community to fill in the training that your leaders need. What matters is that they are being coached and trained. Here are just a few of the coaching options we try to offer:

- Some of our leaders are encouraged to meet regularly with a consultant or coach who is equipped to give them one-on-one assistance to become more effective leaders. Churches without the staff for this kind of coaching may want to bring in outside resources to coach their leaders. While this is not always a necessary strategy for building strong leaders, I have discovered that the men and women who opt to be personally coached usually show potential to be influential leaders beyond the boundaries of one LOLMD group.

- Many leaders attend a small "coaching pod" led by mature leaders. These groupings usually consist of about six people and allow for more personal interaction and deeper challenges. A large number of our LOLMD men's groups meet on Monday night, and these pods meet one hour before that.

- We encourage leaders to take the time to watch coaching videos that I post on our website every week. These are available to any leader from any other church as well. My Journey Group stays one week ahead in our curriculum so that I can walk the other leaders through their upcoming meeting step-by-step, giving them options for questions to ask and ideas for how to lead their groups.

- Finally, our leaders are strongly encouraged to attend our larger Leadership Community series.[16] This is a gathering of leaders that meets on Sundays for training and some interaction. This level of coaching can be replicated by just about any church of any size. It doesn't depend on sophisticated or costly resources at all. The instruction is geared toward the more basic topics our Journey Groups address, but it doesn't stop with generic questions like how to lead a discussion or how to deal with someone who talks too much and dominates the group. It is "in-the-flow" training that addresses deeper issues like how to help people become who they were meant to be. Also, we often offer weekend training sessions that touch on specific topics for our leaders. We try to expose them to as many opportunities as possible to hone their skills.

Before moving on, I have a couple of final thoughts about coaching for you to think about. First, note that I used the phrase "strongly encourage" when referring to the training for our coaches. None of our coaching or training is mandatory. That said, our leaders and staff are rather persuasive on this point both in what they communicate verbally and in modeling the truth that none of us ever outgrows our need for training. A pastor or leader of a smaller church might read what I've suggested—especially the suggestion that you hire a coach—and say, "This is way out of our price range. We can't afford that kind of outside involvement and intense coaching." I understand your reaction. But when you built your building, did you hire an architect? Did you use a builder who contracted out for specific tasks like wiring, plumbing, and flooring? I'll bet you did. Perhaps your church has raised funds in the past. You struggled with fundraising until you hired a consultant, and you were surprised by how much you *didn't* know about fundraising. Expert coaching can often mean the difference between building a sound structure and building one that falls below acceptable standards. We're talking about the infrastructure for the leadership culture of your church. It might be worth considering if it's time to bring in some outside help.

The Selection Process

We're getting down to specifics now, and one question you might be asking is, How do your groups come together? What exactly does the selection process look like? Though some people sign up and their names are given to a leader to set up interviews with them, ideally they come out of previously developed relationships. But I'll share with you my own pattern, one I've developed over many years of leading groups. You may find it frustratingly vague, but it's been quite reliable. First, I begin praying, three to four months before the advent of a new group. I pray for open eyes and a ready heart. I ask God to put people in my path, to help me build a connection with them. If I've led someone to Christ that year, they are an obvious possibility. Months of prayer infuses me with a sense of anticipation. Whenever I interact with people, I find myself wondering, Is he someone God is bringing to my group?

Next I schedule one-on-one meetings with any of the guys I feel might be good candidates for the group. At these meetings, I'm not concerned about testing their spiritual depth, but I do look for signs of spiritual hunger. I want to see a deep yearning for the Lord and a desire to grow. If that desire is not there, I've learned to hold off on inviting that person into a group. I will suggest other growth opportunities and make a note to check back the next time around.

If I sense that a person is hungry to grow and he will be a good fit for the group, I ask to meet again. This time, I run him through the headlines of our orientation material. I ask him to take the material home, read over it in depth, pray, and let me know in a couple of weeks if he is interested. Finally, I invite him to our group orientation and ask if he's ready to commit to the group. Once the group begins, members have two weeks to sign a group contract and make their commitment firm.

Relate or Reproduce? A Few Thoughts on Mixed Groups

At Perimeter we have groups for men and groups for women. That's it. And here are the two reasons for that: *vulnerability* and *reproducibility*. We find that you cannot achieve the level of depth that is needed for long-term growth when both men and women are present in a room. For example, imagine asking men in a mixed group of men and women, "How are you doing in the area of pornography?" Not a single man would want to answer that question candidly with women present, nor would the women know how to handle the responses. Some try to solve this dilemma by splitting a larger group into men and women for times of sharing and prayer. Imagine the conversation on the way home. "How was your group? What did you discuss?" I am sure there are some leaders who may be particularly skilled and could pull this off, but I know too many who have tried, and it just didn't work and something was lost. If the goal of discipleship is to produce a woman or a man who is mature and equipped, this will require a level of transparency, authenticity, and accountability that will be more than just a little uncomfortable in a mixed-gender group.

There are several other reasons *not* to have mixed discipleship groups.

Whenever groups include couples or are composed of single men and women, there is a strong need for social interaction. There is certainly nothing wrong with this, but experience has taught us that in a mixed group, the need for social interaction often ends up trumping the higher goal of missionality. We find that couples groups or mixed-gender groups tend to do fairly well for a short season of time, perhaps one year. After that time, something usually happens to disrupt the social fabric of the group, and far too often, the social needs of the group win out over the missional and discipleship goals of the group.

One final problem with mixed-gender groups is the need for consistency and balance in the group dynamics. Let's say a couples group meets for one year, and in that year, one of the men leaves his group. Perhaps his reason is completely benign, such as a shift in his work schedule or a major life change. Where should his wife go for her discipleship growth during the next year? Should we penalize her for something her husband could not help? Or consider a woman who leads a female coworker to Christ (something that should be happening regularly in our groups). It can be very awkward for this new believer to come alone to a couples group, and to bring her husband to join the men would be a formula for disaster.

We'll be the first to admit that the process of discipleship is *never* perfect. There are also problems with having single-gender groups (including the dissatisfaction of many who want the groups to mix more), but in my opinion there are more difficulties associated with mixed groups. While social interaction can be a worthy goal for mixed-gender groups, we recommend that churches pursue the goal of life-on-life missional discipleship with single-gender groups. Other group formats can address the legitimate needs of couples, and they should be pursued outside of the discipleship process. One idea is to offer couples small groups on a monthly basis. This works well, particularly in churches that don't have Sunday night services.

The Finish Line

Every race has a finish line. The finish line determines what the weeks or months leading up to the race look like. Are you hoping to set a personal best record? Everything from the first day of your training until the moment the chip tied to your shoe makes contact with the touch pad at the finish line will reflect how serious you are about that plan.

Here is how we define the finish line: mature, equipped disciples who invest in the maturing and equipping of other disciples. But as great as that statement is, it's still too general for me. I want to know what real maturing and equipping looks like week after week in our groups. From casting the vision for life-on-life, to the curriculum our groups use, to coaching our leaders, we have endeavored to lay out the parameters of the race for every person involved in a LOLMD group. We've discovered that if we don't define the course of the race, people will naturally slow down or wander off track. Setting the parameters of the race doesn't define our finish line — becoming mature and equipped — but it does help us gauge if we are on track to finish the race.

So what is the appropriate course of the race? We've discovered that a well-defined path is necessary if we want groups to reproduce beyond themselves and to have a multigenerational impact. By week three every member is required to sign a covenant, and the covenant sets expectations. No one can continue in the group without signing one.[17] The covenant not only holds an individual to a high standard, it also keeps the group on track as an entity. It asks everyone to honor the precious commodity each member contributes every week: his or her time. Rarely have I had to ask someone to leave a group I was leading because he broke the covenant. But I have made that difficult decision. When one person won't or can't do the homework, attend the meetings, or call when he can't attend, the commitment of the entire group begins to erode. The men who chose to leave were not necessarily spiritually immature or caught in sin; they just had life or career changes that made fulfilling the covenant no longer feasible. The covenant communicates the standard, but the leader holds the group accountable to that standard.

Most groups operate by a "least common denominator" rule: if a leader allows the standard to fall for one member, that level will become the standard for that group. That's why the leader often has to make the call about a particular member bowing out of the group. I know that for some people the word *covenant* is offensive, so please understand that the purpose of a group covenant is in no way punitive. By signing one, the members of the group agree to collaborate toward something bigger than their own personal growth. For us, the covenant that people sign *is* the course we hold them accountable to. If we aren't following that course, it's unlikely we will finish the race victoriously.

The Journey
Part Four

The years had taught Donna to loosen her grip on her daily to-do list. But today she had a healthy respect for the one she'd devised for this week's Journey Group. Last week was sweet, no doubt about it. But there was too much that was too important to miss this week. As she sat in her favorite den chair in the dawning light that morning, she wrote the high points in the margin of Week Four: Grace — How We Embrace the Cross. Keeping the conversation on track didn't come naturally to her, so she prayed for wisdom to direct the women's lively comments toward the all-important themes of today's lesson. And she prayed the women would grasp what it means to be filled with the Holy Spirit. Especially Billie.

A few hours later as the women settled into their seats, Donna reminded them, "If you haven't done your spiritual assessment yet and turned it in to me, be sure to do that before next week."

She knew Patricia and Billie were the only ones left to complete theirs. "I might need some help on this," Billie appealed to Donna but looked at everyone else as if willing to accept assistance from anyone. "I don't know how to answer the questions at all."

"You know, Billie," Patricia said, "I'm having trouble too. Do you want to go over ours together? I'm most excited about yours!"

"Why on earth?" Billie asked. "I'm the newbie here."

"That's right," Donna said, "which means when we take the assessments at the end of the year, you're going to be the 'most improved' hands down."

The women spent a good amount of time going over their memory verses and the Scriptures they had studied. Donna made a few more announcements about events at church and then asked everyone to open their Bibles to Psalm 47.[18]

"We're going to do a little prayer exercise together," Donna told the group. "There are six of us, so we're going to read the first six verses of this psalm out loud. When it's your time to read, mention something about God that you notice in that verse. I'll start, okay?

"Verse 1: 'Clap your hands, all peoples! Shout to God with loud songs of joy!'"

Donna knew the others might not see anything overt in this verse, so she said, "Well, there isn't an explicit statement about who God is here. If you wanted to, you could dig deeper maybe and find something, but for now I'll pass."

It was Patricia's turn. "Verse 2: 'For the LORD, the Most High, is to be feared, a great king over all the earth.'"

Patricia said, "God is Lord and he is the Most High. I've always wondered exactly what it means to fear him. I guess I am learning to fear him because he is the great king over everything and I'm not in control of anything."

Lisa read verse 3: "'He subdued peoples under us, and nations under our feet.'

"Hmm," Lisa said. "I guess this means God is sovereign if he subdues us. He gets the final say, not us, and not even powerful nations."

Allison read verse 4: "'He chose our heritage for us, the

pride of Jacob whom he loves.' " She sat up straighter in her seat. "Oh, oh! I think this means that God chooses our families. Like, he decides who marries who, who parents who. I love this! It means that even though I fail all the time, God chose me as the mother of my child." She stopped and Donna almost directed Heather to read next.

"Wait!" Allison said, with one finger in the air. "I think this also means God is our Father and we have a family line in him too. Right?"

"Right," several ladies responded at once.

Heather read, "Verse 5: 'God has gone up with a shout, the LORD with the sound of a trumpet.'

"Okay if I pass on this one, too?" Heather asked.

Donna noticed that Heather wasn't her normal intensely focused self today. "Absolutely," she answered.

"Except," Heather broke in, "it seems like God isn't just a ruler and all that. He is someone we should celebrate. Even if we might not feel like it?"

"Yes, that's true," Donna said. "Which leads to the last verse we'll read. Billie?"

"Verse 6: 'Sing praises to God, sing praises! Sing praises to our King, sing praises!'

"Weeelll," Billie began, looking a little bewildered by the entire process. "I'm not sure. What Heather said, I guess. If I think about most songs, like love songs, they usually celebrate someone. I guess this means God is worth celebrating ... a lot ... it says to sing to him four times in one verse."

Before Donna could respond, Heather said, "My husband won't sing in public. Or anywhere else for that matter."

"Neither will mine," said Lisa.

"For a long time, neither did mine," Donna said, "but he sure does now."

"What changed?" Heather asked. "I've actually noticed him in church. He kinda stands out, since so many men just stand there with their hands in their pockets during worship."

"Well," Donna said thoughtfully, smiling at the memory,

"Hank didn't sing because he thought it wasn't manly and he thought—mistakenly—that he could sing to God in his head and that would be enough. But one day he realized he couldn't talk to me without opening his mouth. He also kept running into verses in Scripture that commanded us to sing to God. What can I say? He just got over it!

"Now, I know some of you will be tempted to use Hank's story to 'influence' your husbands to quit standing there like driftwood and sing during church, but I caution you on that. Why don't you just let the Holy Spirit work on them and, while you're waiting, pray?"

"I've heard you guys mention the Holy Spirit more than once," Billie said. "What the he—heck is that?"

"Billie, I'm so glad you asked," Donna said. "We're going to take a few minutes to pray the truths we just read and then we're going to talk about the most important thing you'll ever learn in this group. And it involves the Holy Spirit. But first, let's give God some much-deserved applause."

The women, at Donna's direction, put aside their Bibles, notebooks, and coffee mugs and knelt on the carpet at their seats. Although Donna told them not to feel obligated, each one prayed a sentence or two thanking God for who he is, for the truths they had read about him in Psalm 47.

As they got resettled, Donna repeated, "What we are going to learn today is the most important thing you'll ever learn in this group." And then, as if not sure the women had heard her, she added, "I'm not kidding. If you can get this right, you'll get everything else right."

Donna told the women to open their Bibles to Romans 6. She began with a question: "What do you think it means to be filled with the Holy Spirit?"

"To have peace?"

"To understand God's will?"

"Good, but do you think those are benefits of being filled with the Holy Spirit or the actual filling?"

"Oh, I guess they are just benefits," said Lisa.

"So maybe knowledge of what the Spirit has done …," Patricia said, her voice trailing off.

"Surrender," said Allison, "that's what I think it means."

"Good," said Donna, "those two words begin to capture it. Let's look at Romans 6 and see if we don't find a description that puts appropriate surrender together with appropriate knowledge."

"I don't get it," said Billie.

"That's okay. It's deep, difficult truth. Let's read and see what you think."

They read Romans 6 and Donna noticed that everyone's face reflected confusion, not clarity. Billie wasn't the only one. She led them through a clear discussion of the passage, focusing on three pivotal words:

> *Know*: knowledge of who we are in Christ is the first priority. We are dead to our old sin nature. It isn't gone, but we are now separate from it. We were buried, or baptized, in Christ, and we have risen in him.
>
> *Consider*: it is one thing to know something, but another thing altogether to consider it, to make note of it often. To bank on it.
>
> *Present*: we respond to the Lord by presenting our "members" to him. The women discussed at length what was meant in Romans 6 by these members: our hands, feet, minds, hearts, eyes, and so on.

"There is a prayer I pray almost every morning," Donna told the women, "that puts these three ideas together. It goes something like this: 'Father, today I pledge to consider what I know. I died to sin, I was buried, and I have been resurrected with you. And so now, Lord, I present my hands, my eyes, my heart, my feet, my mouth, all of me, to you for your use today. I'm yours.' "

"So how does it work?" Billie asked. "Like, all of a sudden—boom!—you just don't sin anymore?"

Billie's question was asked with searching innocence; otherwise the women might have chortled out loud. Instead, they looked at their new friend indulgently and smiled.

"Don't get me wrong," Donna said, "we definitely have the power to obey. It's just that none of us is perfect. We can make progress, but the truth is there is never complete surrender in any of our lives. That's why we all need to grow."

"So do we just suck it up and obey even if it feels like we can't?"

This time it was Heather who asked with a tinge of desperation in her normally confident voice. The others looked to Donna with a collective "Help!" on their faces, and she couldn't help but love them. They wanted to please, just like most women she knew. Just like me, she thought.

"Actually, that hardly ever works, wouldn't you agree? None of us possess willpower that matches the power of God over sin. I honestly think that when we reach the end of our own capability and cry out in surrender to him, that's when we really benefit from the filling of the Holy Spirit. When we know the truth and surrender to it, acknowledging our own inability to conquer sin."

"I think I get it," Billie said slowly, in a small voice, as if trying out a new language. "Hey, Donna, can you give me a copy of that prayer? I think I understand it now, and if I pray it, it won't be just copying you. It will be just me and God."

"Sure thing, Billie."

They spent the last few minutes of their time talking briefly about what it meant that their group was about more than their own personal growth; it was missional. Allison and Heather piped in with suggestions for ways they could volunteer together every week. The rest of the group registered a barely hidden dismay that they might be required to add another weekly commitment to their already busy schedules.

"Those are great ideas for every once in a while," Donna remarked, "but missional doesn't necessarily mean we do a mission together. It means we hold each other accountable to being on mission where we each live, work, and play. It means asking God to work his mission into our lives naturally and authentically."

"But what about the Compassion in Action weekend next month?" Heather asked. "I'm in charge of one of the projects."

"Great!" Donna said. "Let's definitely do that together. Next week, why don't you fill us in more?"

"Speaking of where we work," Billie said, "can we pray together for David? He has a job interview tomorrow."

And that's exactly what they did.

The Profile of a Leader

It's Not What You Think

O ver the years at Perimeter Church, we've had seasons that intruded into our church life like an unwelcome guest. Those seasons were often short-lived, but while we were in them, it felt as though they might never end. We always felt surprised when the challenges came, and relieved when they passed.

One of the trickiest times for a leader is navigating those surprise times.

During Jesus' ministry, people often responded with surprise to his actions or words. Jesus' words, as familiar as they may be to us, are like no other words we'll ever hear. If Jesus' words don't startle you from time to time, you may want to take a second look at what he has to say. Has his Word coursed into your heart and caused it to expand lately? Has it caught you off guard and amazed you beyond your normal reaction to it? His way is the unexpected, unassuming, unpredictable way, the I-didn't-see-that-coming way. The paradoxes in the parables alone are astounding:

The workers who show up late make as much money as
    those who show up early and work all day.
The wild son runs into the outstretched arms of the father
    while the faithful son turns his back on that embrace.
The smallest seed produces the biggest plant.

And then there is the mystery found in the day-to-day life of Jesus himself:

The widow who gave next to nothing impressed him more
    than the rich philanthropist who donated enough cash to
    fund an entire building program.
Religious leaders were persona non grata to him, but he
    heartily welcomed children as if they were VIPs.
Jesus delayed his arrival so that both Lazarus and Jairus's
    daughter died before he reached them.

When Jesus said, "But many who are first will be last, and the last first" (Mark 10:31), no wonder his disciples reacted. They themselves were, by all accounts, the first. They fancied themselves the next celebrities in the kingdom, the bigwigs who would sit next to Jesus at state dinners. They were his entourage, if not the center, the orbiting epicenter. No wonder Jesus' disciples were not only "astonished," but "those who followed were afraid" (Mark 10:32) when he uttered this backward values statement. It must have taken them by surprise.

At Perimeter, taking our cues from Jesus, we discovered that the "chosen beginnings" of life-on-life discipleship were counterintuitive. We chose real substance over impressive branding. We chose impact over success. We chose small over big. We chose slow over fast. Sometimes we started out on the normal, accepted path first—as in our hare-like haste to launch fast and furious—only to learn through trial and error that there was a biblical alternative. In some cases, it took a long time to discover that our chosen beginnings would ultimately and naturally lead to surprising outcomes.

Lyle, who pastors a church in Florida, once told me that you can tell more about a leader's character by how he responds to *no* than by how he responds to *yes*. Lyle often finds himself saying no to seasoned leaders. As a church planter, Lyle has had the privilege of setting a standard for discipleship at his church from the get-go. When people come to his church having led in significant ways in other contexts, they often assume that their experience qualifies them to lead at his church. But Lyle makes it clear to anyone who wants to be a leader that they need to be discipled first, regardless of their background or experience. He'll frequently tell seasoned leaders, "I'd like for you to go through our discipleship process first." Then he waits to see how they take that news.

I'll tell you more of Lyle's story later, but it's clear to me that he understands that one of the most important characteristics required of biblical leaders is humility. If prospective leaders refuse to submit to a discipleship process or feel that they no longer need that sort of training, they likely aren't the right leaders for his church. But the kind of leader whose heart has grown soft and teachable by allowing the Word of God to break in is the type of leader who can unlock the power of God's Word for others.

Think It Doesn't Matter? Think Again!

Cathy has been leading women in discipleship for seventeen consecutive years. Her perspective on the impact of discipleship is stunning:

"I lead nine young mothers right now, which represents nine marriages (eighteen people) plus twenty-two children. Forty people, total! I get to impact forty people per week by spending two hours on Tuesday mornings teaching a group of moms about Jesus. Isn't that amazing? So I see God use discipleship to change marriages, moms, families. In fact, almost every woman that I have ever discipled is now married, and most have kids, so I could not begin to guess the number of people who have been touched. So cool!"

At Perimeter, we require our prospective leaders to be last before they can be first. We ask that they sign up for a Journey Group and learn to follow before they try leading others. The training and discipleship that occur over a two- or three-year period in a small Journey Group prepare a person to lead in a way that no course or seminar ever could. Great leaders start small— as a member of a small group—before they take steps to expand into the wider spectrum of leadership. They learn what it's like to be influenced before they attempt to influence others. We bring them into the path of leadership by a slow and deliberate route.

For those who view leadership as something they have already attained or as something to achieve, this often comes as a surprise. But when leaders attain the role of leadership by way of discipleship, rather than being appointed based on gifts, skills, or experience, they frequently display two unique qualities that are essential to effective leadership: a humble, willing spirit, and faithfulness. Who wouldn't want a proliferation of this kind of leader in their church? If you disciple your people—and in particular, your leaders—this will happen.

My First Big Surprise

I was a math major in college, and I've been trained to think logically when I encounter a problem or challenge. In many ways, my logical approach has been helpful. But several years ago, someone shared with me a tongue-in-cheek definition of logic that highlights the danger of self-deception: "Logic is the art of going in the wrong direction with confidence." One of the dangers of trusting in our own logical conclusions, rather than in the wisdom of the Word, is that we can often be blind to our assumptions. One of my first conclusions about discipleship was one that I was most certain about. Unfortunately, I later realized I was dead wrong.

New to the pastorate and fresh out of college, I was itching to replicate what I'd just learned about discipleship. All I needed were some men who could benefit from my training. Brad seemed like a natural first choice. He loved the Lord and embodied the old acronym FAT: he was faithful, available, and teachable. I took him out for coffee and asked him if he'd be willing to meet together for discipleship. He responded with a hearty "Absolutely."

"So when would you like to meet?" I asked.

"How about 6:30 on Monday mornings?" Brad said. "That's the best time for me."

"Sounds good," I said with enthusiasm, writing it down in my planner.

I looked up, pen poised, and waited. After an awkward silence, I prompted Brad, "And?"

"And what?"

"And what other two times would you like to meet each week?"

In my college experience, being discipled meant meeting once for study of God's Word, once for doing evangelism together, and once for recreation, for doing life together. I knew that having these regular meetings each week were the way to truly pour my life into another person's life. I looked across the table at Brad and waited eagerly for his response.

"Uh, Randy," he said, "you *do* know I'm married, right?"

"Sure."

Clearly we weren't communicating. "And you know I have kids? A house? A job?"

Well, I knew all that, but that didn't change my definition of discipleship. It seemed we were at an impasse. Brad wasn't willing or able to meet more than once a week, and I wasn't willing to bend on what I believed to be the logical plan for discipleship. I left my time with Brad discouraged and convinced of the conclusion I shared later with a college friend: "You just can't do discipleship after college."

I'm happy to report that I eventually learned from my mistake. Life is demanding. And despite what most students think, life actually gets busier after college. That's why we designed our discipleship process to take into account the challenges of the average person's life.

Remember Lyle, the church planter I mentioned earlier? Lyle

came to church planting with a solid conviction that his church needed to embrace the discipleship model if they were going to impact their community for the kingdom. He started out committed to the inverted funnel of discipleship first, everything else later. "Trust me" is what Lyle continually told his leaders that first year. When you plant a church, people expect you to invest immediately in a children's ministry, in Bible studies, or in the myriad programs seemingly necessary to meet the needs of a burgeoning church. Telling everyone to be patient about these concerns, Lyle started a discipleship group with four other men. His wife started one with four women. He told everyone to hold on while the maturing and equipping of discipleship did its slow, sure work. His example in those early days underscored for everyone the priority of discipleship over everything else. When the two groups ended, ten new groups emerged, led by Lyle, his wife, and the eight men and women from their original groups. Lyle's church is now in its third generation of leaders and groups.

What Leaders Look Like

I think Lyle has it right. Leaders of Journey Groups and of any other initiative or program in the church must have the qualities of faithfulness and a humble, willing spirit. Life-on-life missional discipleship has the capacity to create this kind of leader. It doesn't guarantee anything, but, like the exponential growth of bacteria in a meticulously prepared Petri dish, it provides the necessary environment for one leader to multiply into several. At Perimeter, our discipleship process can take up to three years. Why so long? We'll get to that in another chapter, but one reason is that discipleship is not a factory for cranking out healthy Christians; it is a laboratory for reproducing leaders. That's why Journey Groups at Perimeter are expanding. Life-on-life discipleship produces, within most groups, healthy leaders who know how to replicate the process. Our leadership base for everything else we do as a church is broadening because we no longer recruit leaders; we reproduce them.

Recently, I asked some of our discipleship veterans to share what they believe are the top three requirements for any leader of a Journey Group. I gathered their answers and came up with the following list of characteristics. It's important to note that these traits are descriptive as much as they are prescriptive. Discipleship is not some magic cauldron into which we plop a leader and a group of followers and, after some sizzling and stirring, cook up some mature, equipped leaders. Though we have engineered this process to mature and equip people in the faith, we also recognize that not every person who comes through our process will emerge ready to lead. Some will never lead. And there is no such thing as a perfect leader. But the process can produce mature, equipped leaders who have the following characteristics:

1. A mature, equipped leader leads himself well in his own walk with God, which includes study of the Word, prayer, and a missional life.
2. A mature, equipped leader has a strong, consistent personal worship habit. You can't feed others if you haven't been fed yourself. One discipler said she was surprised and disheartened by the number of leaders who are trying to fill leadership roles in the church (both discipleship and otherwise) without having a consistent personal worship habit.
3. A mature, equipped leader has a humble, teachable spirit. None of us has ever "arrived." The sanctification process is lifelong, and if someone thinks he is ready to lead because he has nothing else to learn, he is probably the last person you want leading a group.
4. A mature, equipped leader leads his family well, including leading consistent family worship and devotional times, practicing healthy marriage principles, and seeking to lead his children to Christ.
5. A mature, equipped leader is available. She exhibits a commitment to give of her precious resources of time, money, and energy so that others may know the Lord better.

6. A mature, equipped leader has depth in the areas of knowledge, skills, character, and vision of the Christian life. This includes adequate training in theology and knowledge of the Scriptures. This doesn't mean that a leader must have all of the answers. Wisdom is more important than knowledge.

7. A mature, equipped leader has had training and/or experience in group dynamics and leadership. One woman remarked that she had been in groups where the leader was a mature Christian but was not equipped to lead group conversations.

8. A mature, equipped leader demonstrates a willingness to be vulnerable, to share honestly and openly about failures and weaknesses.

9. A mature, equipped leader is accountable to others.

10. A mature, equipped leader knows where the group is going, is clear on the group's purpose, and knows where each member is in their walk with God and how to move them forward.

I encourage you to ask yourself this question: Is there a mechanism in your church that has the capacity to create leaders with these qualities ingrained in their character and practices?

I did do something right way back when I asked Brad to spend three times a week with me. Life-on-life discipleship does, indeed, go beyond one weekly meeting. Often it involves a constant flow of communication between the leader and the members of his or her group. But this interaction should take place naturally, outside the boundaries of the regular group gathering. It happens in the context of friendship. And it requires an investment beyond meeting two hours once every week.

You may be familiar with the math in 2 Timothy 2:2. Paul writes, "And what you have heard from me in the presence of many witnesses entrust to faithful men who will be able to teach others also" (ESV). Four generations are represented in this one verse. We see Paul passing on what he has learned and experienced to Timothy, who passes it on to the "faithful men," who are to pass it on to "others also." When Paul's admonition to Timothy is translated into a regular practice—like life-on-life missional discipleship—the exponential possibilities for growth and reproduction are breathtaking.

Let's say Cathy has led a different group of six women, all married, with an average of three children each, for seventeen years. And let's say the duration of each group is only two years. That first group touches the lives of thirty-five people. Then, as these women become mature, equipped wives and mothers, their husbands and children can't help but catch the aroma of Christ in new, transforming ways. Even if these numbers are somewhat inflated, it's hard to deny the trickle-down effect of one leader's life of faithful investing in a few at a time. If just five women, including Cathy, from that first group choose to lead a second generation of groups, that leads to around 175 lives influenced during the third and fourth years. And if four more women from each of those five groups go on to lead groups, that's potentially seven hundred lives impacted in years five and six. If the pattern were to continue, almost three thousand lives would be affected in years seven and eight. Even with the attrition of people and groups that is certain to happen, the potential for ongoing exponential growth still exists.

Where did it all start? With Cathy, or, if you want to look back even farther, with the woman who invested in her. Or perhaps the woman who discipled *her*, Cathy's spiritual grandmother. This is the way the kingdom works; it's how God chooses to grow his church. Discipleship isn't a method or program; it's the God-ordained way of growing the kingdom from small beginnings to worldwide impact. And it happens through the investment of one life in the life of another.

Some time ago, I arranged for a friend to meet a well-known author, speaker, and consultant. My friend had just retired and sold his business. He had plenty of time and resources and wanted to spend them strategically for the kingdom. At lunch with these two men, I sat back and listened as they dreamed about the next phase of my friend's life and what his work might look like. It was pretty impressive to hear them talk, and I had no doubt that some of their ideas could actually move from dream to reality. Toward the end of our time together, the well-known author asked me, "Randy, what's your input? What do you think your friend ought to do in the second half of his life?"

I had to think for a moment. I didn't want to sound dismissive of their ideas, but I felt that I had to answer honestly. My response wasn't as dramatic as several of the scenarios sketched on the napkins before us, but I was convinced that it represented the most powerful opportunity for my friend's life to have kingdom impact. I looked at my friend and said to him, "I think the best way to invest your life for the kingdom is to select a few men and pour yourself into their lives. Help them become mature, equipped followers of Christ. After you send them on their way to lead other men, choose a few more and start the process again. If you want to get to heaven and be greeted by thousands upon thousands of men who owe much of their spiritual relationship with Jesus to you, this is the best plan I know."

I am wholeheartedly convinced that one individual seed — one disciple — dying to self and investing in the life of another person has the greatest impact on eternity. A tiny seed has the potential to touch more people than the largest cathedral could hold within its walls, more individuals than a TV broadcast could transmit to with a thirty-minute segment, more lives than just about any megachurch initiative could ever hope to reach. All it takes is one leader, offered up as a living sacrifice, taking last place, moving ahead in small, slow, and unimpressive steps.

To Pastors and Church Planters

We dub a fool a silly goose and refer to a futile pursuit as a wild-goose chase, and when we're in trouble, we tell others that our goose is cooked. Despite all of this disrespect for geese, they have something to teach us about leadership.

Scientists used to assume that migrating geese fly in a V for-mation because it is the most efficient way to fly. But years of study have shown that there is more going on. When geese fly in formation instead of flying solo, their heart rates lower, their visibility increases, they are aerodynamically placed to glide using less energy, and they are able to communicate with each other more freely. They can cover up to 70 percent more distance than when they fly alone.[19] The other geese fall in line behind the head goose and determine their placements in the V according to his position. They take their cues from him.

I like to think of the senior pastor as the head goose. The pastor charts the course, leads the way, and absorbs the turbulence. When it comes to the spiritual formation of the church, he is the one whom members of the church follow.

What does that have to do with discipleship? To quote my friend Carter, a pastor in Nashville, "If discipleship is a disease,

A Pastor Talks about Discipleship

Recently Carter, a pastor and discipleship leader, showed up at 6:00 a.m. on the nose for his men's group, and he wasn't the first one there. These guys couldn't wait to meet together every week. And often when they finished, Carter would exclaim that his hair was on fire because the time was so rich and meaningful.

I asked Carter to share what he loves about life-on-life discipleship:

He gets to watch men connect their life stories with Jesus' story. They move out of their small stories into his big story.

He leads best when he "gets out of the room" and lets them teach each other from the Word and their experience.

His preaching has been enhanced.

His intimacy with the Lord has deepened.

In Carter's mind, he can't afford not to do discipleship.

then somebody has to start the disease, and that somebody is the pastor. And the pastor will need to do it for the rest of his life."

Just so I don't overstate the role of the lead pastor, I'll add that when the head goose gets tired, he should fall back and allow another goose to slip into the leading role for a spell. There are seasons when he might need to step away for a time, but more often than not, successful discipleship in a church begins with the senior pastor and his example.

As you read these words, please bear in mind that I am not writing them from some ivory tower. Like some of you, I have planted a church. Like many, I have struggled to find the right programming that will produce healthy growth. It is a constant battle to filter all of the information that comes flying at us as pastors and leaders and to prioritize the thing that holds the most potential for authentic growth. Monthly budgets and weekly attendance are our constant companions, but the return on a discipleship investment dwarfs the simple addition of another program. So I encourage you not to lose heart.

How is all of this possible for a busy pastor with a congregation, a family, a denomination, a schedule overflowing with meetings, weddings, funerals, baptisms, sermon preparation, date nights, kids' events, and maybe a little time for a run at the park or a golf game every now and then? How does time meeting with a small group and discipling them fit into all of this?

It really is simple. But simple doesn't mean easy.

Not If, but What?
The Importance of Curriculum

Everyone uses a curriculum. Don't believe me? Take a straw poll of leaders of small groups, asking them what they do, and listen to what people say.

"We just pick a book of the Bible and do an inductive study."

"We share our needs and challenges and pray for each other."

"We follow the same general outline every week, but the specifics vary."

"Our denomination provides material that we use."

"We choose a book by a Christian author on a subject we're all interested in." (Hmm, maybe you're reading *this* book in your small group?)

Whether you use predigested material or you have developed a fairly involved plan of your own, you use a curriculum. Just meeting to pray? That's your curriculum. Studying a book together short-term? That's your curriculum. Letting the Spirit lead your meetings? That's your curriculum.

The word *curriculum* originated in the 1600s as a derivative of the Latin word for "course," specifically a course for a horse or chariot race. That's a far cry from the stuffy academic flavor the word carries today. Before it was used in formal education, *curriculum* referred to the necessary stages of development children go through on their way to adulthood. And before it evolved into a rigid syllabus of assignments and tests, a curriculum was a series of tasks and experiences designed to take someone on a journey toward maturity. So in this sense, everyone uses a curriculum. Even if they say they don't.

This chapter is not a marketing tool for the curriculum we have developed at Perimeter, a program called *The Journey.* It is, instead, a challenge to examine your curriculum. What do you use to facilitate the spiritual growth and discipleship efforts of the people in your church? Did you choose it thoughtfully? Is it designed with a clear purpose in mind? And, most important, does what you currently use satisfy that purpose? Has it been tested and tweaked several times either by you or by its designers? Is it haphazard and inconsistent, like so many varieties circulating out there?

When we work with a church to launch life-on-life missional discipleship, we don't "sell" them our curriculum, but we do strongly encourage leaders to craft or choose a curriculum that fulfills the goal we established: "Life-on-life missional discipleship is laboring in the lives of a few with the intention of imparting one's life, the gospel, and God's Word in such a way as to see them become mature and equipped followers of Christ, committed to doing the same in the lives of others."

Can you disciple people without a curriculum? If by curriculum we are referring to a clear, methodical plan that covers most essential topics and enables someone to follow Christ toward maturity, then yes, I suppose you could do all of that without a *formal* plan. But I don't recommend that, and here are several reasons why.

> *Without a careful curriculum your discipleship won't be reproducible.* Have you ever met a marginally equipped leader? I sure have. Once the training wheels of the mentoring

relationship are taken off, this kind of leader is a disaster.
He no longer has a reliable guide to help him, and he
fails to learn from the modeling he observed as a group
member. We must recognize that not every leader learns
by example. Some need more than just the experience
of being a member of a group to prepare them to lead.
A curriculum fills in these gaps and makes the ongoing
training smoother.

Without a curriculum your discipleship won't get better. If your
plan for growing people to spiritual maturity is forever
shifting or stuck in a cycle of reinvention, how can you
measure success or failure? How can you make the right
adjustments? A curriculum allows leaders and groups to
track their progress.

Without a curriculum your discipleship won't be intentional.
Have you ever prepared poorly for a talk or a sermon?
How much freedom did you feel you had to adjust that
talk or sermon to your audience or to a change in your
flow of thought? How confidently, naturally, and coher-
ently did you speak? If you've ever hurriedly prepared a
message, you know that your confidence in delivering
that message drops. When there is no plan, your mind
is continually preoccupied. This isn't a safe environment
for leadership because the leader isn't free to lead; he is
typically locked in reactionary mode, responding to what
comes at him next.

*Without a curriculum your discipleship won't be able to man-
age the expectations of the group.* A curriculum tells the
group what they are doing and, if it's a good curriculum,
why. It lays out, in a linear progression, the direction
the group is going. Without a curriculum, the rules can
change; the plan can swerve off track or come to an
abrupt halt. No curriculum equals no security for the
members of the group.

These are a few of the reasons for the use of a carefully prepared curriculum. But most important, it must be a curriculum

that is gospel- and Christ-centered and rich in sound historic and biblical theology.

The Journey to *The Journey*

Do you remember my friend Brad? The one who had the audacity to use his family and his job as his excuse for not meeting more than once a week? Well, I did get one thing right back then, even though my expectations were slightly unrealistic. The discipleship patterned for me in college was designed to paint a healthy, *complete* picture of discipleship. The truth is that most of us favor one method of discipleship over another. Our esteem or disdain for certain curriculum probably reflects our methodological preferences. Some of us like things to be engineered—the more complex and controlled, the better. Others of us prefer a more organic approach. We'll cite all the agrarian references in the New Testament as proof that growth should occur naturally, without much concerted effort. The truth falls somewhere in between these two perspectives, yet both are necessary and valuable.

My suggestion to Brad that we meet three times a week beautifully accomplished the marriage of both of these perspectives. My plan was that our first meeting would be devoted entirely to content, engineered, while the second two meetings would be devoted to our lives, the more organic side of discipleship. If a leader leans too heavily on engineered methods, she will try to use the curriculum without any of the nuances that are bound to occur in a discussion among unique individuals. This leader, if not careful, will fail to recognize the unique needs of her group and will fail to respond to God-ordained circumstances and situations. On the other hand, if a leader leans too far toward the organic, he likely will discard any set direction, and the group quickly will lose focus. When this happens, people don't take the curriculum very seriously. Group members will draw the conclusion that the vital topics you are trying to cover really aren't all that vital.

I began to develop a curriculum that I could use with the men I hoped to disciple even before we moved to Atlanta and planted

Perimeter Church. At the time, I knew that any curriculum I developed would need to embrace both the engineered and the organic approaches. I also understood that the goal of discipleship — to produce mature, equipped followers who can produce mature, equipped followers — also had to be the goal of the curriculum. After years of refinement, the plan we now use is far more than a simple curriculum. It is a training tool.

When I first wrote the curriculum, I thought through all the issues I felt men and women needed to cover in order to grow spiritually, and I formalized those topics into a one-year curriculum. The first time I used the curriculum, I took five guys through it, and we repeated it again for a second year. The second time around, we added five rookies to the group. The veterans, who had already been through the study, didn't stick around because the material was that good; they stayed because of the relationships. Invariably, when I asked them which year had the most impact on their personal spiritual growth, they responded that it was the second year, the year of repeating the curriculum. I kept hearing the same thing: "I think I began to get it the second year." I know this: every three years when I come back to the same content, I am reminded how badly I need it.

When we began discipleship as a wholesale movement in our church, we continued to use the one-year curriculum and allowed group members to repeat it a second year. But as great as the material was, I still felt that we were leaving out too many important topics. So I visited an isolated cabin to pray, think, and plan with the goal of reworking our discipleship curriculum. I wrote out topics on individual sheets of paper and spread them on the floor, using three basic categories to organize them: systematic, biblical, and practical theology. I knew that we wanted to train people in all three categories, in a balanced way.

The floor of my cabin was a massive quilt of white paper. I systematically arranged the subjects and assigned a certain number of weeks to each. Then I did a quick tally of the total and came to the alarming conclusion that to equip people effectively in each area would take eight to nine years! That wasn't practical, so I went back to those sheets of paper on the floor. I went through the heart-wrenching task of cutting one week here, two weeks there, one topic here, and one subtopic there, and eventually whittled the subject matter down to a three-year plan. This plan formed the basis for the curriculum we use today, a plan of study known as *The Journey*.[20]

Regardless of your background or history, no one ever outgrows a need for the basics. Vince Lombardi's famous one-liner, delivered every year in the preseason to his Green Bay Packers players, makes this point well: "Gentlemen, this is a football." It is impossible to grow and meet the goal you set unless you keep returning to the basics.

I have a friend who tells an interesting story about his high school basketball team. The coach became ill during the first week of the season, so another teacher was pressed into service as coach. Unfortunately, he was not a basketball player and had never coached basketball before. The team already had a pretty dismal track record, and with a less-than-average team and an inexperienced coach, there wasn't much hope for a successful season. The fill-in coach admitted he knew nothing about basketball, so he asked the players—who were more experienced than he was—what they typically did at their practices. Because it was the first week of the new season, the team was still just working on fundamental drills. So that's what they did. Over and over. Day after day. They kept practicing the basics until they knew them so well they could perform them in their sleep. They didn't learn anything new or sophisticated. At one point, the team became frustrated with the monotony of their practices, but neither they nor the coach had an alternative plan. So they kept at it.

Would it surprise you to learn that this team went on to win the state championship?

In the spirit of training in the fundamentals, our curriculum covers the same material in the first six weeks every year. This section, called "Gospel Living," covers the fundamentals of the Christian life. Even though I have used this content for more than forty-five years, I find that I still need what these first six weeks bring into my own life. To give you a taste of what we cover during this time, here is a list of the subjects that make up the fundamentals:

Week 1: Glory — Why We Embrace Christ: Finding the Missing Piece That Satisfies

Week 2: Glory — How We Embrace Christ: Embracing Christ in Personal Worship

Week 3: Grace — Why We Embrace the Cross: Learning to Rightly Relate to God

Week 4: Grace — How We Embrace the Cross: Embracing the Cross through Spirit-Filled Living

Week 5: Truth — Why We Embrace the Word: Following God's Plan to Glory

Week 6: Truth — How We Embrace the Word: Living as Ambassadors to a Broken World

The first six weeks also establish the five foundational areas that we will build on in every meeting for three years:

Truth: what God has revealed for his people to know, understand, and obey.

Equipping: massaging God's truth into life so that it becomes understandable and usable.

Accountability: asking the hard questions to encourage living fully for Christ.

Mission: engaging with the lost world in order to impart the gospel through word and deed.

Supplication: engaging in conversation with God to express dependence on him.

Establishing a Rhythm

Members of our Journey Groups commit to being in the group for one year at a time. The schedule follows the school year, with four months off in the summer and four weeks off at Christmas. While some of our leaders find this time off disrupts the continuity of the group, we have observed that too many groups lose traction when people have to skip meetings during busy times like the holidays or can't make a meeting because of family vacations. No one is pressured to participate longer than a year, and we don't frown on those who quit after one year. Life circumstances sometimes render another year impossible.

After the end of the second year, most leaders take stock of their group to determine whom they want to encourage to continue for a third year. They explain to the members of the group that the third year is especially designed to prepare leaders, and that by committing to a third year, members should understand that they are also committing to lead a group in the very near future. Often I will ask one of the third-year men in my group to lead with me. By leading alongside me, he picks up the hands-on leadership skills he needs as he watches a seasoned leader for an entire year.

At the end of the third and final year, it is usually obvious who is called to lead a Journey Group and who is not. Not everyone is comfortable with or interested in leading adults, so we encourage those people to consider discipling children or youth. The good news is that I've yet to see someone who, after three years of maturing in our Journey process, is not able to lead a group of adults, youth, or children.

Our curriculum is not a tidy, complete package. After all, I jettisoned five years' worth of material when I created it! But those subjects weren't simply relegated to the shredder. Over time, we designed ways to use them to supplement the core material. We offer frequent seminars throughout the year to augment the material covered in the weekly meetings. When members sign up to be involved in a Journey Group, they agree to attend at least one of these seminars each year. In these sessions, we cover subjects that require deeper study and are often too complex for the typical lay leader to address. The three seminars we commonly offer try to answer the following questions:

How do we know the Bible is God's Word?
How do we learn to share our faith?
How do we discover our spiritual gifts?

We also use retreats to give people a chance to engage in some of the more involved tasks in the discipleship process, such as designing and documenting their life plan. This is an important exercise that doesn't fit into the time constraints of a weekly meeting, nor is every leader equipped to guide people through this process.

Retreats and seminars are opportunities for group members to fill in the gaps in their spiritual training. They also allow those who hunger for more to go deeper without leaving the others behind. Our seminars and retreats also communicate our support

Not for Everyone

A member of our church recently said to me, "Randy, I have a friend I'm thinking of inviting to be a part of my Journey Group, and I'd like your input."

It turned out that this man's friend was in an unhealthy place because of a crisis in his life. He was suffering from an abusive background and an addiction was dominating his life. For many of us, the knee-jerk reaction would be to invite him in: "By all means, welcome him in. Give him the benefit of your attention and the embrace of the group." But is that the wisest course of action? We have learned that it's not always best to invite a person with certain addictive struggles into a group setting. This can be a mistake, both for the person in question and for the group. Those who are trapped in addictive patterns or who are battling chronic fear or depression may need a support group that is designed especially to meet their needs. If your church doesn't have groups like Divorce Care or Celebrate Recovery, it would be wise to find similar resources in your community or through other churches. The most important thing you can do for someone like this is to point them to an appropriate place to heal, while keeping a supportive relationship with them.

to our leaders. We are saying to them, "You can't do it all, and we don't expect you to."

You, More Important Than *What*

When Jackie and her husband were missionaries in Brisbane, Australia, one of the first young women Jackie encountered was Carly. When they met over pepperoni pizza on Carly's first day of her freshman year in college, little did either woman know what transformation would take place over the next two years of their relationship. When Carly talks about her discipleship, she calls it Jackie. That's because discipleship, for Carly, *was* Jackie:

> Jackie taught me how to have a quiet time by modelling it and even sitting in on one with me. She taught me how to study the Bible for myself, without a book to help me. She taught me how to share my testimony, how to share the gospel, how to manage my time, how to identify my spiritual gifts, how to meet with and lead other girls. This godly lady wanted to see me become a mature disciple of Christ, not just a convert, or an infant tossed about by the waves and wind. She earnestly wanted to see me be a strong woman of God, fully assured of my position in Christ and totally desiring to see others won to him too. She wanted to see me blossom into a Christian woman producing fruit for the growth of God's kingdom.
>
> I am a very social person; I have many friends who love and care for me. But her love was on a spiritual level. She didn't just want me to be happy and healthy; she wanted me to be spiritually mature. What she did—the time she invested in me, and the interest she took in my Christian walk—was nothing new or innovative. She didn't invent a new method; she simply followed after the Master's example. She followed Christ.

Carly's description of discipleship could never be described by saying, "We did [blank] curriculum together." What Jackie did with Carly was reinforced and passed on by who Jackie was. We call our model life-on-life because the curriculum is simply the tool. If Jackie had not been living out the lessons she was teaching, those lessons would have lost their credibility and some of their power. Carly, who is now a wife and mom and a discipler of women herself, eventually would have sniffed out the discrepancies. She might have become skeptical and disillusioned. When all is said and done, the person discipling *is* the curriculum for the person being discipled. The life of a person — living by grace, trusting in the gospel, committing to the study of Scripture and prayer, and modeling what it means to follow Jesus Christ — is the best curriculum you will ever find. God has been using it to change lives for more than two thousand years, and it has a proven track record. We certainly aren't going to improve on that!

The Journey
Part Five

Something was up with Heather. Last week, Donna had sensed it, and this week she was fairly certain the other women did too. Heather usually bristled with energy, and although she could be abrupt, she typically wore a look of settled contentment on her tanned face. But today was different. Something was definitely up.

"Let's stop and spend some quiet time praying together," Donna said, interrupting the lively flow of conversation that had followed the women from the kitchen to the living room. Donna knew that as the weeks progressed and these women became comfortable, trusting friends, the energy of their social interaction would be, on occasion, a deterrent to their pursuit of spiritual growth. She didn't want to burst the bubble of their camaraderie, but she did want to steer them toward an even deeper need than friendship: a close relationship with Christ.

"Lord, you are *here*, with us. That's amazing. We're honored to have you here, and we want to listen to you, to respond to you." Donna paused and then added, "Let's be quiet and wait on the Lord for a minute."

In the stillness, she sensed Heather, who sat next to her

this morning, squirming in her seat. She prayed silently, "Lord, would you give me wisdom about Heather? I know I can't call her out, so would you lead her to open up and be transparent about what's really going on? You know her heart and her circumstances, Lord. Make me sensitive to her."

After they paired up and recited John 8:31–32 to each other, Donna asked, "How many of you have completed your Twenty-One Days of Worship?"

Amid some groaning, Heather said softly, "I have."

The women broke into spontaneous applause that clearly embarrassed Heather, so Donna said, "Great! We'll all get there eventually. Remember, this is all about function, not form. The main goal is not to check off twenty-one days—although we're impressed, Heather—but to meet with the Lord."

Donna led the group through their study, finding they had questions that made the discussion lively and encouraging. As their leader, Donna was aware of the need to massage the truth into usability, so she asked a question to take the discussion even deeper.

"What is something you used to believe but you no longer believe now?"

"That my husband is supposed to meet all my needs," Patricia said.

"Yeah, me too," Lisa agreed.

"Wait," Billie said. "You mean they don't? But your husbands are believers. I kind of thought if David—when David—becomes a Christian, then he will be my leader. He'll become the kind of husband I need. That isn't true?"

Donna looked to Patricia and said, "Want to address that? It's a great question, Billie."

"Sweetheart," Patricia began, "I know it seems like that's the way it's supposed to be. Remember the counterfeit glories we talked about a few weeks ago? Well, we can make our husbands into idols. Our children too. It's just that they are flawed like us. Only God can meet every need. Only God. If we try to make our husbands into gods, they'll always disappoint us."

Heather got up with a muffled "Excuse me" and left the room. They heard the click of the bathroom door down the hall.

"Here's another question," Donna said. "Why do you believe what you believe?"

Donna strove to pay attention to the answers while listening for Heather's return.

"To be honest, some of it is because someone I trust told me to."

"I read it in the Bible."

"I just feel like it's true."

"How about this one," Donna said. "What is the difference between a belief and a conviction?"

"Well," Allison responded, "before I became a Christian, I actually believed in Jesus, sort of. But when life got hard and I met people who sneered at that belief, I discarded it. Now, under the same circumstances, I know I'd hang on to him. I'm convinced. So I guess a conviction is something you are committed to with all your heart. A belief is more casual."

"That's good, Allison," Donna said, pulling out a legal pad from beneath her Bible. "I'm going to explain something about the way we view life that, I think, will give us one reason why we believe what we believe.

"There are basically two worldviews, ways of looking at the world: naturalistic and theistic." Donna wrote the two words on opposite sides of the paper. "The naturalistic view says that the world was not created, that there is no real truth, only reason. In fact, the naturalist would say she depends on reason to understand life. The theistic view says the earth was created by God and that God gives us truth. The Christian understands that Ethan, here" — Donna patted Ethan's chubby leg lightly enough that she wouldn't wake him — "is a miracle of a Creator God."

"Hmm," Billie said, "I know this might seem basic to you all, but I have lived my whole life as a naturalist. That's exactly what David is right now. He thinks he can figure out all of life with reason."

"Yes," Allison added, "but even though I'm a Christian theist, I sometimes think I have to figure things out myself. When things go wrong, even little things like a fight with my husband or dealing with a colicky baby, I think it's my job to reason out the solution. But if my view of the world is theistic, I can't rely on my reason alone."

"That's true," Donna said. "Our human reasoning is flawed. Let's look at two passages we read this week."

Patricia and Lisa read the passages out loud. "For as the heavens are higher than the earth, so are my ways higher than your ways and my thoughts than your thoughts" (Isa. 55:9 ESV) and "There is a way that seems right to a man, but its end is the way to death" (Prov. 14:12 ESV).

"Can anyone else talk about a way you have viewed the world from a naturalistic point of view and how that impacted your life?" Donna asked.

"I can," Heather said. She had slipped into her seat just seconds before. "I know I was supposed to talk about a project for us to do together. I'm sorry."

"It's okay," Donna said softly, and several others echoed her, leaning forward in their seats, ready to listen.

"I just ... it's ... you know something's wrong, so I might as well tell you." And then Heather allowed the tears to flow. As she sobbed, it seemed something heavier than tears fell away from her face. Lisa went to the kitchen and came back with a box of tissues, which she laid gently on Heather's lap. Patricia sidled closer on the couch and with the tenderness of a mother placed an arm around Heather's shuddering shoulders.

"Mark got a DUI two weeks ago," she blurted. "I was so ashamed, I couldn't tell you. Ashamed and angry and hurt. I've been reasoning it out for two weeks, trying to figure out how to fix it, to fix him. I've just been getting angrier and angrier. I don't know if you know, Donna, but he called Hank and told him right away. He is getting help and he's so sorry. I've never seen him so broken. But I haven't been able to forgive him. I asked him to keep it quiet, since he ... he embarrassed me so much."

Mark was in Hank's Journey Group, had been for two years. Donna, of course, had not heard a word, and she assured Heather of the fact. Hank would not betray the confidence of "his guys" for the world.

"In the bathroom just now," Heather said, "I just stood there behind the door and listened to you all. And then I realized it. I am basically a naturalist. Sure, I do the disciplines and I believe, but my beliefs aren't convictions. I am sick of relying on me, on my strengths and my reasoning to get by. This isn't going to work unless I change how I view the world . . . my world. I'm desperate to get God back on the throne where he belongs. I don't care who knows about Mark now; that's his story to tell, and if it helps him he can tell it. I don't think reasoning will ever get me to the place where I can forgive him. But I suspect that God can. Yeah, I have hope; for the first time in two weeks, I have some hope."

"Heather," Donna said after a pause, "we are going to hope with you. That's what prayer is."

"But prayer is also being honest with God," Patricia added, "so it's okay if you want to express exactly how you feel about all of this to God, either with us or by yourself. You have permission to do that, Heather."

"That's right," Lisa said. "Goodness knows Patricia and I have ranted about our families with each other. Well . . ." She stopped and considered her words, looking to Patricia for affirmation. "We didn't exactly complain about them as much as express how we *felt* as truthfully as we could. I can't tell you how much that helped."

"Thanks, everyone," Heather said. "I'm sorry I took up so much time. We're supposed to cover mission, right? Did I preempt that?"

"No," Donna said. "I want us to surround you with prayer and then we'll take our last five minutes to go over mission before we leave."

The women prayed longer than their remaining five minutes, but no one minded. When they were finished and had passed the tissue box around the room, Donna said, "One final question. Does anyone have a quick update on what they have experienced this week in missional living?"

"I called my friend Callie about going to lunch," Allison said. "No response yet."

"That's great, Allison! That took guts."

Lisa said, "We decided to kind of 'adopt' the boy next door. He's seven and has a single mom who works all the time. He plays soccer, so we went to a game last week. Tom even went along and is spending time tutoring him and kicking the ball around in the front yard. It's cool to see Tom care about someone like that."

"Lisa, that's awesome; that's what missional living is all about. I want to add that all of life is ministry. Folding towels, making breakfast, getting the neighbor's mail — these things can be beautiful expressions of God's glory when we do them in the power of the Holy Spirit for the glory of God. I know it sounds too simple, but it's true. What little things do you do all the time that can become missional? If we are change in his pocket, then God can spend us whenever, wherever, and however he wishes. Think about that this week."

Pandemic
The Power of Multiplication

In October of 2011, scientists extracted bacteria from the teeth of medieval corpses discovered beneath high-rise office buildings in London's financial district and determined that the pathogen they had found was the forerunner of all modern plagues—the bubonic plague, more commonly known as the Black Death. In the fourteenth century, the bubonic plague killed an estimated one hundred million people worldwide and reshaped the economy, culture, and government of Europe. Historians believe it took one hundred and fifty years for the population of Europe to fully recover from the effects of the plague.

Pandemics must originate somewhere. In the case of the Black Death, it most likely was brought to Europe by merchants and explorers who had visited China. Plagues are never static. They tend to migrate, as the Black Death did along the Silk Road on its way to Europe. And they tend to last a long time. The bubonic plague, though never as virulent as it was in that first global outbreak, is still present today. Wherever and whenever a pandemic occurs, it leaves an indelible mark. Plagues travel quickly, and they bring death and disease to all that they touch. Plagues have the power to change our lives as individuals. They can even change the direction of an entire nation.

Let's imagine what it would be like if a plague had positive effects instead of negative ones. What would an outbreak of *health* look like? For starters, we'd need fewer doctors. Fewer tissues to dry tears. Fewer insurance policies. There would be greater productivity in the workplace because sick days wouldn't be necessary anymore. If wellness were transmitted like disease, living cell to living cell, everyone would want a bite from *that* bug.

Well, believe it or not, that bug exists. Life-on-life discipleship is a "health virus" just waiting for the right conditions to cause a pandemic, and it is God's answer to the death and brokenness that plague this fallen world.

Addition

Tim had the misfortune of opening two new restaurants just before 9/11. Optimistic about the future, he hired two guys to help him run them, and his new employees were quickly drawn to his infectious love for Christ. Then, in the wake of the towers' falling, Tim's restaurants both failed. The money he had invested in them evaporated. But what was left when the businesses failed was something far more valuable: two former employees who were in a new relationship with Jesus and were taking steps toward maturity in their walks of faith. Tim jokingly tells the men, who work for him in another business venture now, that their salvation cost him a whopping three hundred thousand dollars apiece. But he quickly adds that it's a price he'd gladly pay again.

Tim sees his business failure this way because his priorities are in the right place. Tim has owned successful restaurants in Atlanta for thirty-three years. The product of a broken home, Tim had himself gone through a painful divorce and by age forty was reluctant to commit to the woman he had been dating for five years. That's when Tim got infected. Immediately after inviting Christ to rule his life, he met a man who discipled him and invited him into a Journey Group. Within three months, Tim was involved in the church and had gained a fresh sense of confidence. He asked his girlfriend to marry him, and they have been married now for more than eighteen years. Both he and his wife are leaders of Journey Groups now. Tim will tell you of his great desire to see young men become godly husbands and fathers. He has committed his life to giving his disciples the tools he never had. Tim oversees forty-seven employees, and he has ample opportunity to invest himself in their lives as well. He sees the men and women who work for him as his spiritual responsibility.

Tim operates his business with a readiness to share the life-changing truth of the gospel with anyone God places in his path. Tim knows that God's saving grace can germinate and grow at any time in someone's life. One of his employees, a seventy-two-year-old waitress who had worked for him for twenty years, had endured much pain and suffering. Tim knew about her struggles and simply loved her. One day she came to him and said, "Tim, I'm not saved, but I want to be." Tim gave her one of Perimeter's "Life Issues" booklets and a Bible. Not long after that, she gave her heart to Christ.

That's addition. When God brings someone to Tim, he will share his faith and present the gospel. And often another believer will be added to the church.

But Tim knows that as wonderful and important as the work of addition is, when he leads men to maturity in the faith and equips them to lead others, his impact reaches even farther. He and his wife have been leading groups for more than fifteen years. And many of the people in those groups have gone on to lead other groups. After fifteen years, it's impossible to quantify their reach.

That's multiplication.

And Multiplication

A man once approached me at a conference in Orlando. "You led so-and-so to Christ and discipled him, right?" he asked.

"That's right."

"What you probably don't know is that that man led me to Christ and discipled me. And I discipled a guy named ..."

I won't mention the man's name, but I will say that most of you reading this would know his name and be aware of his national and global impact. Thousands have been influenced by his preaching, teaching, and leadership. Our discipleship lineage has a wider reach than anything else we can do for the kingdom.

If the leadership of our church said to me today, "Randy, you have to choose between continuing in the pastorate as a preacher or discipling men life-on-life. You cannot do both," I wouldn't think twice about it. I'd give up the pastorate. That's not because I don't love pastoring. I do. But I am keenly aware that discipleship has the greater kingdom impact. The power of discipleship is such that over an average lifetime, anyone — a pastor, staff leader, or layperson — can touch thousands of lives. If you simply meet with two guys for one year and have those two guys

In and Out

Although multiplication is a dramatic chapter in the discipleship story, there are some commonplace ways to help your groups multiply. One simple tip I've learned over the years is to make sure a few new people come into the group each year as the third-year members exit——hopefully to start new groups. Instead of eroding the consistency of the group, this practice emphasizes several key things. First, it makes for a more missional culture. New people require the group to make a special effort to include and assimilate others. Second, it keeps the group from gravitating to that old "we don't want to give up our comfortable group" mentality that often sets in when a group has met together exclusively for a long time. Finally, it encourages leadership. The "old" guys see their responsibility to lead the "new" guys. In fact, I always enlist coleaders in our last year together.

disciple another two guys, and then figure in the influence on their wives and children, you begin to see the power of multiplication. When this simple habit of discipling people is repeated year after year, the potential to impact lives is phenomenal. Even with normal attrition (because no one bats a thousand), it is possible to impact several thousand lives. Just imagine meeting a few thousand people in heaven whose lives were impacted by your steady faithfulness year after year in discipling others to turn around and disciple others. The power of multiplication is stunning.

Infecting the Church with a Spiritual Health Virus

A healthy church will grow. I'd go so far as to say a church cannot be healthy and *not* grow. I'm not necessarily talking about getting bigger; I'm talking about getting healthier. I hesitate to write much about church growth because there are so many *wrong* reasons to grow. Some want to see their church grow because they long for financial security or success and approval from other pastors or the people in their congregation. There are numerous ways to grow a church in size: by amassing believers from other churches, focusing on felt needs, expanding facilities, offering new-and-improved products, branding a church carefully, and choosing celebrity leadership. Not all of these are wrong, but if they are the primary focus, they can become an idol in the church.

So what are some of the good ways in which a church should grow?

- By being contagious where we live and work and play.
- By serving and loving the community.
- By practicing attractive, healthy worship.
- By praying and fasting.
- By multiplying through individuals and small groups.

Most discipleship efforts fail because they focus on addition. They rely on a few gifted leaders who add spiritual value by attracting a core small group whose members are attracted to their leadership. But this kind of discipleship fails to multiply.

A healthy church is a "two-story church." A one-story church, to use Ken Blanchard's jargon, is one that directs and delegates. Most churches teach their people and then send them out on mission. But LOLMD doesn't stop there. It builds a second story on top of a one-story church. It adds the necessary elements of coaching and support, thereby helping the people who have been directed—taught the Word—to engage their mission.

My good friend Bob says that what happens in life-on-life discipleship is both beautiful and predictable. Bob and I met on the tennis court more than twenty years ago. A friend of his encouraged me to get to know him and share the gospel with him, so I took him to lunch and did just that. When Bob came to faith, he joined my Journey Group, where he grew into a leader of other men. He now coaches leaders. He is a living example of the multiplication power of one life invested in only a few other lives at a time. When he says what happens in a Journey Group is predictable, he knows what he's talking about.

First, according to Bob, men learn to trust. They learn to trust their leader. They learn to trust one another. And eventually they learn a radical trust in a trustworthy God. This doesn't happen immediately, but it often happens more quickly than you'd think. Bob observes, rightly, that men today are programmed not to trust, to be guarded and in control. The new experience of trusting someone is a doorway to a deeper experience of growth.

After trust has been developed, the men become more transparent. Bob remembers a successful but shy executive who joined one of his groups. For the first two months, this man hardly looked up when asked a question, and he never prayed out loud. He never smiled. Slowly, one little step at a time, this man opened up his heart. He had been in Bible studies, but he had never experienced the kind of vulnerability he experienced in this group. Once he got there, however, there was no turning back. Now he is leading his own group, and though it sounds like a small thing, he smiles. Often.

Transformation takes place after men learn to trust and be more transparent. People start changing. Followers become leaders. The immature become mature. The inexperienced become equipped. And when we finally have a means of growing men and women who trust God and each other, who are transparent about their struggles, and whose lives are being transformed, we are ready to infect the world.

Sometimes the best place to start is in the community where God has placed us.

Where Do We Hang Out?

In his lifetime Peyton has attended countless Sunday school classes, Bible studies, and small groups. And nothing, he insists, has been as fulfilling for him as the experience of life-on-life missional discipleship. He admits, "Randy, I don't know of anything else I do where I am as absolutely sure that I'm doing God's will as I am about this."

After three years in my Journey Group, Peyton did exactly what was expected of him: he started his own group. But he did it with a twist. Peyton and eight other guys asked each other, "What is our unique market? Where do we hang out?" and "Where do we encounter unbelievers on a regular basis?" These eight young men were all involved in the business world, and they all played golf at the same athletic club. And so they began their first Journey Group right there at the club. The following year, two groups had formed, and in these groups they had two men who assisted them in leading the group. Both men understood that they would be forming their own groups the following year.

That was ten years ago.

Peyton estimates that in that ten-year period around sixty to seventy men have been discipled. At least ten men are now trained to lead groups. Seeing the fruitfulness of her husband's discipleship with men, Peyton's wife copied the process and has impacted close to sixty women through discipleship.

Peyton says the men he encounters are searching for satisfaction, and life-on-life missional discipleship shows them where to find it. These typically are men who in their early years had embraced the success culture of the business world and now have found it wanting. They have experienced firsthand the disappointments of the market, and they know that money cannot be counted on to deliver their dreams of achievement, financially or otherwise. They are ripe for the gospel, many of them for the first time in their lives. Peyton went to high school with some of the men who populate his group. He has been delightfully surprised by their response to God's Word. The results he sees are not the only reason he continues to disciple men, however. "What we've been doing here will last," he says, speaking of his Journey Group. "It's eternal. I know it counts."

Genome to the Globe

An epidemic is classified as a pandemic when it goes worldwide. At Perimeter we have a global outreach arm of ministry, and it too has been infected by the LOLMD virus. Several years ago, some church leaders in Tanzania remarked to one of our mission

Take a Risk

Peyton's experience can be translated into some very practical wisdom for multiplying your influence through discipleship:

- Find an affinity group, people with whom you share a common interest.
- Make sure the men or women who lead are trained and theologically sound in their teaching and practice. But take a risk on the number two person who leads with them.
- Create an authentic environment where every person is assured that you're all in the same boat.

volunteers, "We've noticed something different about the people you send over." We knew what had stamped the image of Jesus so deeply, so indelibly, so noticeably on the lives of our people that others would sit up and take notice. And so we told the leaders in Tanzania about our Journey Groups.

After we shared our discipleship process with them, they had just one question for us: "Can you teach us how to do it?"

The transformation of our mission work in Tanzania to an LOLMD model didn't happen overnight. Nor did it unfold quickly when we began to apply it to our existing partnerships with churches in Bangkok, Warsaw, or the other global cities where we were engaged in cross-cultural ministry. Now, however, every new partnership we make is built on this foundation. In Sao Paulo, in Johannesburg, and in Dublin, the foundation for our mission work is life-on-life missional discipleship.

We are not going into all the world promoting our "box" of materials. Instead we are stimulating an awareness in the minds and hearts of our partners that there may be a better way to bring people to maturity in their faith. Not a new way, but without doubt a forgotten way. So as we partner with different leaders around the world, we recognize that their contexts are different from our own. We focus our efforts on the principles that transcend culture. As a result, leaders have stopped stumbling from one program to another and instead invest in the lives of men and women to produce mature and equipped disciples. If we have this right and the foundation is truly Jesus' method and model, ministry in any culture becomes more than just another program.

We have discovered that people everywhere long to connect with the biblical Jesus, whether they play golf in suburban Atlanta or live in the shadow of Kilimanjaro in Tanzania, whether they wait tables or play the stock market. And we know that Jesus wants to connect with us. He wants to be the primary influence in our lives, through the work of the Word and the Spirit. The LOLMD model is simply a biblical and effective means of stimulating the spread of the gospel genome across every barrier. Yes, the gospel is unrivaled in its ability to transform the human heart. But the power of the gospel, present in the Word of God, is best translated from one life to another. As men and women hide the Word in their hearts, giving it time to germinate and grow, the fruit of their lives can be enjoyed by other believers. Mature Christians who rely upon the power of the gospel can pass along what they know and experience to those who are hungry to grow in their faith.

Life-on-life. It's the key to the exponential power of the gospel.

The Journey
Part Six

Even if I had presented these fictional accounts as fact, you probably would have suspected that they were fake. Deep relationships don't often form this quickly, growth doesn't usually happen this smoothly, and prayers are not always answered this neatly. Composites are like that. They wrap reality up in tidy packages. But I compressed the drama of a three-year LOLMD Journey Group into six abridged meetings because I want you to see the potential, to dream a little. Let's look in on Donna and her group one last time. And let's go straight to two conversations that reflect both the hope and the healing that discipleship has to offer.

This time, Heather didn't hide anything. One look at her face, and Donna knew she'd been crying the entire drive from her house to Lisa's. She also knew that Patricia and Billie had each taken a meal to her. Lisa had texted encouragement every day. Allison had written a good old-fashioned note. Heather was hurting, but she wasn't hurting alone.

"I couldn't wait to get here today," Heather said to the

women once they had all settled into their places in Lisa's cozy living room. Allison wasn't there, but she had called Donna to tell her she was running late.

"Tell us about your week," Donna said, sensing that Heather needed to talk.

"Mark isn't doing well at all," Heather said, "but the funny thing is, I'm doing a lot better. You know how we had to write out a definition of the gospel this week?"

Heads nodded, but no one knew where Heather was going with this.

"And then we had to summarize our own experience?" she said without waiting for a response. "I have been a Christian for so long, it was hard at first. I know I shared my journey, but I have to admit it was surface. This week I thought a lot about the fact that God saved me when I wasn't looking for him. I like to be in control, but my salvation was all his doing."

By this time the tears on Heather's tanned face had dried and she smiled. "I don't know why, but thinking about that comforted me. I thought, 'If I can trust God for my eternal destiny, surely I can trust him for this.' "

Donna knew Heather might have more to say, but she didn't press her. They all heard Allison's tap on the door, followed by her cheerful "Yoo-hoo!"

"Heather!" Allison bent to wrap her friend in a long embrace.

"Go on, Allison," Heather said with a grin, "tell them your news."

Donna smiled and nodded.

"Well," Allison said, catching her breath, "remember my friend Callie? Donna and I had lunch with her and Donna shared the gospel and—"

"Be honest, Allison," Donna said, "all I did was get the conversation started. You did the rest."

"Or God did, right?"

"Right. Keep on."

"Before I could even get all the words out," Allison said,

"Callie said she had been feeling like something was missing in her life. Marriage wasn't it. A new baby wasn't it. It was Jesus!"

Donna said, "Callie prayed the tenderest prayer asking Jesus into her heart."

Allison added, "I was thinking about Christmas and our party next week. I couldn't ask for a better present, you know?"

Billie, who was already crying quiet tears of joy, said, "I know how you feel. David is starting to ask about God. Without my prodding him at all. For him to accept Jesus is all I want."

"I was so mad at Mark," Heather said, "but now I just want him to be right with God. Really right. He's more disappointed in himself than I am. And he has a group like this to support him. Thanks for praying for him, but for me too."

Donna said, "Why don't we pray together?"

Billie nodded and said, "Yes, let's do that. I think I'm catching on to this prayer thing."

The Forgettable Model

And the Unforgettable Life

Today, if you visit the sixteen-acre site in New York City where America sustained the largest loss of life from an attack on our own soil, I guarantee you will not think about the model the architects built before the actual 9/11 Memorial came into being. That visit will commandeer your senses. And any questions you had about the *how* of its construction will be replaced with the impressive *what* of it all. Your ears will fill with the sound of rustling leaves — or the creaking of bare limbs if you visit in the winter — as you make your way through the grove of oak trees in the plaza. Before you see it, you'll hear the water pouring into both of the massive reflecting pools. Once you reach the waterfalls, your eyes will surely become riveted to the list of names, almost three thousand of them, inscribed in bronze at the edge of those pools. In the museum, you'll see the "Wall of Faces," designed to communicate the colossal scale of human loss. Chances are, if you take a trip to the 9/11 Memorial, you won't stop by the preview site next door on Vesey Street where the architect's model is still on display. Why, when you can see the real deal?

I began this book talking about models. And I hope you quickly forgot all about them as you continued to read. Models, the good ones, embody something so unforgettable that all memory of the miniature structure fades once the form and function it foreshadowed are realized. But allow me to take you back there one more time.

A Model Transformed or an Idol?

In chapter 1, I suggested that the model is the servant to its intended purpose. I reviewed the most recent models of church, the *attractional* and *influential*. The attractional model has enabled the church in recent decades to present itself to its community and culture with relevance. It has taught the church to speak the ever-evolving language of its environment. In its best forms it has made the gospel understandable without compromising its meaning. The pastoral/attractional model has fused the best of our traditions as a church with a necessary focus on relevance. Meanwhile, the influential (or missional) model has challenged the church—a body made aware of and alert to its surroundings by the attractional model—not only to communicate the gospel effectively within its walls but also to live it and share it outside those walls. You might say the evangelical American church had begun to suffer the effects of the aging process: a minor stroke here, a hardening of the arteries there, a little arthritis, and a general slowing down of its life. Both of these models provided the necessary rehabilitation for the church to reengage its message and mission with its milieu. Important purposes.

So why are the models so visible? Why do we, pastors and leaders, talk about them so much? One reason, I suppose, is that we are the architects. We value the *what* of church—its ultimate health and ability to glorify God—but we care a lot about the *how* too. As leaders, we may never fully forget our models. We built them, after all.

But models are tricky. To those of us who, by necessity, have to think about them more than others, they can become something they were never meant to be: idols. Even the best of them.

One of the most intriguing models I've ever read about was the one God instructed Moses to make while his people were wandering in the desert. The bronze serpent was far more than a symbol; it was a model with a mission. The Israelites were dying left and right from snake bites. Dying, I might add, because of their sin. Moses crafted a metal image of the very thing that represented death — a snake — and held it up in the air, and all who turned their eyes toward that snake lived. After the crisis had passed, Moses put the bronze serpent on display in the tabernacle. Solomon moved it to the temple. And there it stayed, gathering dust, for eight hundred years. At some point the serpent ceased to remind people of God's intervention on their behalf, and they began to worship the reminder instead of the Rescuer. In a bold move, King Hezekiah, who must have decided enough was enough, "broke into pieces the bronze snake that Moses had made, for up to that time the Israelites had been burning incense to it" (2 Kings 18:4). And that was the end of the serpent.

Or was it? Jesus resurrected the old symbol to proclaim himself the ultimate healer of sin and giver of life. In a statement that makes no reference to the tainted history of the bronze serpent, he said, "Just as Moses lifted up the snake in the desert, so the Son of Man must be lifted up, that everyone who believes in him may have eternal life " (John 3:14 – 15). That's what Jesus does. He breathes life into the model. He transforms it.

You have just read an entire book devoted to the design and dimensions of the life-on-life model. We at Perimeter have spent years being blessed by it. I'm convinced life-on-life missional discipleship is an essential, God-given way to connect the people in our churches to the gospel, to the glory of God, and to the ongoing mission of the church. But without the transforming breath of Jesus, it is just a model. The day our particular version of discipleship ceases to point people to Jesus Christ will be the day it becomes an idol. And if that day comes, I hope to be the first to tear it down.

What Survives

Among all the other trees at the 9/11 Memorial stands one with a unique history. It is called the Survivor Tree. First planted in the 1970s, it was plucked from the rubble at Ground Zero, its trunk blackened and its roots snapped off. In 2001 it measured eight feet tall. A local nursery tended it until it was replanted at the memorial in 2010. By then it had grown to thirty-five feet.[21] It seems only fitting that a tree that survived that infamous day symbolize the resilience of our nation after the 9/11 attack.

This is the question all model makers must ask: will what I have built survive? I propose that the model is never what lives on. According to Paul, we are construction workers of *life*. And the lives we build must sit firmly on the living foundation of Jesus Christ:

> For we are God's fellow workers; you are God's field, God's building.
>
> By the grace God has given me, I laid a foundation as an expert builder, and someone else is building on it. But each one should be careful how he builds. For no one can lay any foundation other than the one already laid, which is Jesus Christ. If any man builds on this foundation using gold, silver, costly stones, wood, hay or straw, his work will be shown for what it is, because the Day will bring it to light. It will be revealed with fire, and the fire will test the quality of each man's work. If what he has built survives, he will receive his reward. If it is burned up, he will suffer loss; he himself will be saved, but only as one escaping through the flames.
>
> Don't you know that you yourselves are God's temple and that God's Spirit lives in you? If anyone destroys God's temple, God will destroy him; for God's temple is sacred, and you are that temple.
>
> — *1 Corinthians 3:9–17*

Paul understood that when Jesus told his disciples to build houses on rock instead of sand, he wasn't referring to models; he was referring to life.[22] If you really look at Jesus, the models fade and that life comes into focus:

- "In him was life, and that life was the light of all men" (John 1:4).
- "But whoever drinks the water I give him will never thirst. Indeed, the water I give him will become in him a spring of water welling up to eternal life" (John 4:14).
- "I am the bread of life" (John 6:35).
- "I give them eternal life, and they shall never perish; no one can snatch them out of my hand" (John 10:28).
- "I am the resurrection and the life" (John 11:25).
- "I am the way and the truth and the life" (John 14:6).

The bronze serpent has been dust in the wind for almost three thousand years now. Before that, although it was obviously a God-given symbol, it was just a metal object. But Jesus, who was lifted up on a cross, buried in a tomb, and rose to tell about it, is alive. And he lives on in holy, human temples. He survives in us. *He* is unforgettable.

Where from Here?

Beginning the Journey

N ow for the hard part. It's easy to read about and even think about life-on-life missional discipleship, but how do you get started on the journey to establish it in your church?

If you are not the pastor of your church, perhaps you could give this book to him. Share your desire to be a part of a life-on-life movement, and tell him you're willing to help in any way possible. If he shows no interest, you can always invite a handful of less mature believers to be a part of your own Journey Group. Few good churches would ever forbid such a thing. Then slowly multiply over the years until the fruit of your labors becomes leaven that pervades the whole. Church leadership will notice — probably with delight — growing numbers of mature and equipped believers. Who knows what might happen then?

The following advice is directed to church pastors interested in birthing LOLMD in their churches, but you, the individual church member, will find much that is applicable to you in your setting and in your role as a lay leader. Please don't give up the dream. Pray for it. Fight for it. Do whatever it takes to be a part of life-on-life discipleship.

Here's a four-step process to get church pastors started on the journey:

1. Evaluate Your Situation

This is how it all got started with me. As I've mentioned, I like to find a quiet place just to think for an extended period of time. I remember as a kid walking in on my father alone in a room. He asked me to come back later unless it was an emergency. That made no sense to me, so I asked him what he was doing. His response: "Thinking." I left asking myself, "What does he do when he thinks?" It seemed like a waste of time, and I just knew I'd never do that.

But now I understand. I truly believe thinking is a lost art. We know what it is to like to read, but not to think. But what a profitable exercise it is.

Most people assume they are not as insightful or creative as they really are. Granted, some are more wired for creativity than others. My observation is that thinkers are not necessarily readers, and readers are not always thinkers. Personally, I'd much rather create an idea than read someone else's ideas. But regardless, just like nonreaders need to read, nonthinkers need to spend time thinking.

Spend the first portion of your thinking time evaluating your church's ministry as well as your own. Be brutally honest. Ask yourself questions. Then listen to your answers. "Are we excelling in making mature and equipped followers of Christ? Are our small groups truly helping our people in their spiritual formation? Is our leadership pool increasing or staying the same, or even perhaps shrinking over the years?"

Once you've done a thorough enough evaluation to determine where you are, it's time to start figuring out where you need to go and how you plan to get there.

Now it's time to dream your dream.

2. Prayerfully Dream Your Dream

This really isn't a different step; it is merely a continuation of the first. You're still thinking, but now you're asking God to birth within your heart the right dream.

I wrote earlier that your dream is a vision that reflects the heart of God. And though it shifts and sharpens over time, it is from God. Therefore your dream must first and foremost glorify him. God's church needs leaders, and leaders need dreams.

God-given dreams don't emerge overnight. In my experience, dreaming takes long periods of time, time spent praying and asking God to reveal a vision.

I like to ask God for a dream or vision that is so beyond me it would be doomed to failure unless he is in it. I believe that I should never ask whether a dream is possible; rather I should ask whether it is the will of God.

Then I start writing down all of the ideas I have that I believe *could* be from God. I'm mature enough to know that not everything I write down is necessarily from God, but I have to assume that some of those ideas may well represent his desire and will.

Now it's time to start praying that God would burn his will so deeply into your heart that it becomes a conviction, a persuasion so strong you believe it would be wrong not to attempt it.

This dream or vision should bring into focus the target for your ministry. Now you know where to aim. The only question that remains is, "How will I hit that most important target?"

3. Choose or Design Your Model

In chapter 1, I suggested that models marry dream to function and that the pastor is a model maker. He may be more of an adopter of a model than a creator of one, but whatever model he uses must have his fingerprints all over it.

I also mentioned in chapter 1 that function is the how-to that connects the big, noble dream to real, flawed people. Though it's important to customize one's model, at some point one has to decide which model category it will come from — pastoral, attractional, influential, or life-on-life. (And by now you know my opinion on which one you should pick.)

To a considerable degree, this decision will come down to one's use of small groups. Will they focus on knowledge transfer or life transformation? Will everyone in the group prepare or only the leader? Will they demand a high commitment for participation or allow attendance with no cost to the participants at all? Will group members be selected or can they merely sign up? Will the time together be spent in teaching, prayer, caring, and sharing, or will the focus be on truth, equipping, accountability, mission, and supplication? What size group? Large or limited to no more than eight or ten? Will the groups produce community or seek to mature and equip the members? Will the groups be for believers only or will they include interested non-Christians? Will they be gender mixed or only for men or women? What about the leader's role? Will he or she be a teacher, a disciple, or a coach and mentor? Will the groups have a missional requirement and commitment or focus solely on the needs of the participants? Will the expectation of its members be fellowship or leader development?

It is important to distinguish the differences between small groups and LOLMD groups. (See appendix 4.) I certainly hope you don't hear me belittling small groups. I believe they are very important. We certainly benefit from them at Perimeter.

Over the years we have seen churches consider three options when contemplating LOLMD groups. One option is to cancel all existing small groups and replace them with LOLMD groups. Bad idea! Why kill a good friend?

The second option is to take the format of LOLMD (or even the curriculum of Journey Groups) and use it in a typical small group. Though this is not a bad thing, our experience is that this approach will not produce the same results as LOLMD.

The third option is the one that seems to benefit churches most. This approach is to keep the existing small groups intact and to celebrate their strategic contribution to the overall mission of the church. Then, in a quiet, covert, and nonprogrammatic way, start only one or two male and female LOLMD groups.

Remember, you are sowing a few seeds that will later bring a great harvest. As these two types of groups exist alongside of each other, a symbiotic relationship develops. One group provides community and connection, while the other produces more mature and better equipped followers of Christ.

Once you have identified the target and put a plan in place, you might think it's time to release the arrow. But that is not necessarily the case. Just as athletes, business people, and growing Christians need coaching and support, so do churches in their endeavor to launch a movement like LOLMD. Though there are exceptions to this rule, in my opinion there aren't many.

4. Acquire Needed Resources

Most everything we attempt to do requires resources. Our bodies need the energy supplied by the calories in food. Spiritual obedience requires the power of God's Spirit appropriated through the faith supplied by God's grace. The church is no different. When it comes to birthing a LOLMD movement, a church often needs outside resources.

Let me illustrate. Several years ago a new pastor of a very well-known and respected church called and asked to meet for lunch. This man is just a few years younger than me, but far more intellectual, articulate, and educated. In addition, he is a very godly, humble man. He had heard about discipleship at Perimeter and wanted me to tell him more about it.

It took me an hour to explain what we do and how we do it. I gave him our Journey curriculum, and he asked permission to use it to begin Journey Groups at his church. I was thrilled by the request. I truly felt I had told him most everything he needed to know. I knew he was an exceptional man and assumed he could figure it out.

But I had failed to practice what I preach. How many times have I quoted Ken Blanchard? "One thing you never want to do is to go from directing to delegating. If you do, you create disillusioned learners." And I had done just that to my new friend.

Within a few months, I received a call from this pastor. His first words were, "I can't do it."

"Do what?" I asked.

"Do LOLMD."

I should have anticipated his next words: "Because I've never had it done to me."

He then asked if he could join my group for one year, promising to take what he learned firsthand back to his church. After an enjoyable year in my group, he told me, "I can do it now. Now I understand LOLMD."

Because of examples like this, and because we know from experience that conferences alone don't allow the coaching and support necessary to seed a movement, we began developing resources for those new to LOLMD.

Through the years, we have learned that there are four phases in the process of birthing LOLMD. We have tried to provide the necessary resources to help leaders through each phase.[23]

The first phase is "Envisioning." In this phase, the right conversations take place to enable the church's leaders to think through the principles, costs, benefits, et cetera of LOLMD.

The second phase is what we call "Establishing." This phase includes clinics that are interactive, challenging, and practical. The follow-up from the clinics provides clear action steps for the church team to accomplish before the next clinic. There are four sequential clinics available. Pastors and other leaders receive coaching and support through Learning Communities and Leadership Coaching so that real progress can be made. Once a church has completed the Establishing phase, we're hopeful that the DNA of the church has already begun to change.

Some churches, at this point, sense a call from God to become a catalyst to help other churches in their community to do the same. These churches enter into the "Equipping" phase to prepare them to help other churches go through the Envisioning and Establishing phases.

Now they are ready to move into the "Empowering" phase. These churches begin to take full ownership of their own life-on-life movement. They become centers where churches in their community and beyond can come to get the resources they need. By this time, Perimeter is well out of the picture.

To put all of this in a table would look something like this:

Envisioning	Conversations	Thinking
Establishing	Clinics, Community, Coaching	Being
Equipping	Coaching	Doing
Empowering	Center	Sharing

For those churches that use *The Journey* curriculum, I have made a coaching video available for each lesson, including the orientation I give for all new Journey Group participants. *The Journey* can be subscribed to on an annual basis. Feel free to search for these and other resources at *www.lifeonlife.org/insourcing*.

One Last Thought

After reading all of this, you may be thinking it sounds too complex and complicated to accomplish in your context. In certain respects, I guess it is. As I write this, I'm about to begin my forty-sixth consecutive year of laboring in the lives of a few. And to this day I'm amazed at how steep the learning curve still is. It seems like I learn more each year than I did the previous year.

But let me say that it is certainly worth it. There are many things we choose to do regardless of the cost. Most of us opt to be parents, knowing full well what a difficult, not to mention complex and complicated, endeavor *that* is.

Even so, those who succeed in any complex endeavor in life succeed because they have found a way to keep it as simple as possible.

For instance, to parent well, I've always believed that one must focus on three things: Love your God, love your spouse, and love your children (giving them what they need, not necessarily what they want). Love covers a multitude of sins. As complicated as parenting is, show me a parent who does these three things well, and I'll show you a blessed child.

Likewise, in following the Lord, I suggest one focus on three things: First, be a sincere worshiper; worship God weekly in corporate worship and daily in personal worship. Second, be a faithful disciple maker; constantly mix it up with lost people, seeking eventually to share with them the love of Christ and the hope of the gospel. Notice that I said faithful, not fruitful. God determines the fruit. Just be faithful to be his messenger. And third, be an effective disciple trainer. Always have a handful of men or women whom you are laboring to take to spiritual maturity.

When it comes to training disciples, keep it simple as well. If nothing else, find two people a year who are not as far along as you are spiritually, and invite them into your group. Always have a few leaving each year and a few new ones coming in. Find a balanced curriculum of truth to use and then simply and honestly show them who you are and how you got where you are. Do that year after year and watch what happens. I predict you'll leave a legacy in the lives of so many people that heaven will be filled with citizens who were directly or indirectly impacted by your life.

Could there be anything better?

Journey Group Member Covenant

In order to glorify God by pursuing this opportunity to grow in spiritual maturity and equipping, I covenant together with this Journey Group and commit, with God's help, to the following:

❑ *To attend all meetings, unless providentially hindered.* If I am unable to attend, I will call my Journey Group leader as soon as possible and take responsibility to find out what was missed in my absence. As much as my schedule lies within my control, I will arrange work and other commitments so as not to conflict with Journey Group meetings.

❑ *To be prompt in attendance.* I understand that this group will meet each _____ from _____ until _____.

❑ *To engage in daily personal worship.* This includes a commitment to spend time in prayer and Bible reading in order to grow in my relationship with God.

❑ *To complete all homework assignments to the best of my ability.* I understand that this will usually require about two hours per week, not including time spent in personal worship.

❑ *To participate in group discussion and activities.* I will be ready and willing to give an account of my spiritual progress on a weekly basis for the purpose of accountability for greater spiritual growth.

❑ *To protect the confidentiality of my group.* I pledge to keep whatever is shared in this group confidential so as to encourage trust, openness, and honesty.

❑ *To pray for nonbelievers within my circle of influence* and to seek opportunities to win them to Christ through word and deed.

❑ *To attend at least one weekend equipping seminar during this ministry year* that will improve my skills, knowledge, or leadership abilities.

I understand that the term of this group is for one year.

Signature: _____

The Journey

Master Curriculum Three-Year Overview

Blue Year		
Section	**Module**	**Unit**
Orientation		Orientation
Gospel Living	First Six Weeks of Each Annual Curriculum	1. Glory—Why We Embrace Christ: Finding the Missing Piece That Satisfies
		2. Glory—How We Embrace Christ: Embracing Christ in Personal Worship
		3. Grace—Why We Embrace the Cross: Learning to Rightly Relate to God
		4. Grace—How We Embrace the Cross: Embracing the Cross through Spirit-Filled Living
		5. Truth—Why We Embrace the Word: Following God's Plan to Glory
		6. Truth—How We Embrace the Word: Living as Ambassadors to a Broken World
Grace Commitments	A Commitment to the Local Church	1. The Local Church, Part 1: A Needed Authority for Kingdom People
		2. The Local Church, Part 2: A Safe Home for Kingdom People
		3. The Local Church, Part 3: A Mission to Nonkingdom People
		4. The Local Church, Part 4: An Equipping Station for Kingdom People
Knowing God	The Supremacy of God	1. The Sovereignty of God: Limitless Power, Perfect Knowledge, Absolute Authority
		2. The Spirituality of God: Transcendent, Omnipresent, Immanent
		3. The Immutability of God: Unchangeable, Eternal Perfection

Healthy Marriage	Understanding Your God-Given Roles	1. Male and Female: How God Designed Your Spouse
		2. Headship and Submission: How God Designed Marriage
		3. Love: How Husbands Fulfill Their Role in Marriage
		4. Respect: How Wives Fulfill Their Role in Marriage
Biblical Worldview	Our Place in God's World .	1. The Truth about Science and the Bible: Which Truth Should You Believe?
		2. Before the Design: There Was a Designer
		3. The Facts of Life: Did Darwin Get Them Right?
		4. The Image of God: Why You Are More Than Just a Smart Mammal
		5. Knowing Your Place in God's World: Seeing Yourself through the Designer's Eyes
		6. The Sanctity of a Life: What the Gospel Says about Human Value
		7. What in the World Are You Doing? Fulfilling the Purpose for Which You Were Designed
God-Honoring Parenting	Making Your Home All It Was Meant to Be	1. Your Home as a School
		2. Your Home as a Hospital
		3. Your Home as a Mission
		4. Your Home as a Church

For additional materials and supplemental resources:
http://www.perimeter.org/insourcing

Green Year		
Section	**Module**	**Unit**
Orientation		Orientation
Gospel Living	First Six Weeks of Each Annual Curriculum	1. Glory—Why We Embrace Christ: Finding the Missing Piece That Satisfies
		2. Glory—How We Embrace Christ: Embracing Christ in Personal Worship
		3. Grace—Why We Embrace the Cross: Learning to Rightly Relate to God
		4. Grace—How We Embrace the Cross: Embracing the Cross through Spirit-Filled Living
		5. Truth—Why We Embrace the Word: Following God's Plan to Glory
		6. Truth—How We Embrace the Word: Living as Ambassadors to a Broken World
Grace Commitments	A Commitment to Generous Living	1. Generous Living Is an Evidence Of: Your Level of Contentment
		2. Generous Living Is an Evidence Of: Your Choice of Investment
		3. Generous Living Is an Evidence Of: Your Motive of Worship
		4. Generous Living Is an Evidence Of: Your Demonstration of Faith
Knowing God	The Triunity of God	1. The First Person of the One God: The Father in Whom, and for Whom, We Live
		2. The Second Person of the One God: The Son through Whom We Live
		3. The Third Person of the One God: The Spirit Who Lives in Us

Healthy Marriage	Before and After You Say "I Do"	1. The Myths about Marriage: It's Probably Not What You Think It Is
		2. The Mystery of Marriage: The Search for Oneness
		3. Avoiding the Fatal Attraction: The Best Hope of a Lasting Love
		4. When You Encounter a Stalemate: Living in a Relational Logjam
Biblical Worldview	Living in a Fallen World	1. The Descent into Depravity: Why We Need a Redeemer
		2. The Consequences of the Fall: Sin and Misery in a Broken World
		3. Running from Temptation: Pursuing Righteousness to Avoid Sin
		4. Accepting Suffering, Part 1: How God Is Involved in Your Pain
		5. Accepting Suffering, Part 2: Waiting for Deliverance from Pain
		6. Accepting Suffering, Part 3: The Christian's Response to Pain
		7. Not of the World, but Sent into It: Living as Christ's Followers in a Fallen World
God-Honoring Parenting	Guidelines for Parenting	1. Adopting a Balanced Philosophy: Discovering God's Motive and Goal in Discipline
		2. Applying a Balanced Philosophy, Part 1: Principles of Instruction
		3. Applying a Balanced Philosophy, Part 2: Principles of Preventive Discipline
		4. Applying a Balanced Philosophy, Part 3: Principles of Corrective Discipline

For additional materials and supplemental resources:
http://www.perimeter.org/insourcing

Red Year		
Section	**Module**	**Unit**
Orientation		Orientation
Gospel Living	First Six Weeks of Each Annual Curriculum	1. Glory—Why We Embrace Christ: Finding the Missing Piece That Satisfies
		2. Glory—How We Embrace Christ: Embracing Christ in Personal Worship
		3. Grace—Why We Embrace the Cross: Learning to Rightly Relate to God
		4. Grace—How We Embrace the Cross: Embracing the Cross through Spirit-Filled Living
		5. Truth—Why We Embrace the Word: Following God's Plan to Glory
		6. Truth—How We Embrace the Word: Living as Ambassadors to a Broken World
Grace Commitments	A Commitment to the Lord's Day and His Sacraments	1. The Lord's Day, Part 1: The One Day in Seven Pattern of Life
		2. The Lord's Day, Part 2: A Sabbath Made for Man
		3. The Sacrament of Baptism: The Initial Sign of the New Covenant
		4. The Sacrament of the Lord's Table: A Promise, a Picture, a Memory
Knowing God	The Goodness of God	1. The Righteousness of God: The Standard of Moral Perfection
		2. The Love of God: For All People and for His People
		3. God's Forgiveness: Priceless, Costly, and Free

Healthy Marriage	Learning to Resolve Conflict	1. Embracing a Spirit of Reconciliation: What the Gospel Has to Do with Resolving Conflict
		2. Ten Rules for Resolving Conflict: Demonstrating a Spirit of Reconciliation, Part 1
		3. Ten Rules for Resolving Conflict: Demonstrating a Spirit of Reconciliation, Part 2
		4. Ten Rules for Resolving Conflict: Demonstrating a Spirit of Reconciliation, Part 3
Biblical Worldview	Redemption from a Fallen World	1. Justification and Adoption: God Will Never Condemn His Children
		2. Assurance of Salvation: Knowing to Whom You Belong
		3. Sanctification: How God Makes His People Holy
		4. Glorification: The Destruction of Death and the Perfection of God's People
		5. The Second Coming of Christ: The End of the Age
		6. The Millennium: The Present Reign of Christ
		7. The Final Judgment and New Heavens and Earth: Fulfilling the Promise of the Gospel
God-Honoring Parenting	Engaging Your Child's Heart	1. Focusing on the Right Target: Influencing the Heart of Your Child
		2. Understanding the Competition: Dealing with Cultural Influences
		3. The Power of Parental Influence: For Better or for Worse
		4. Will I See My Children in Heaven? What Every Parent Longs to Know

For additional materials and supplemental resources:
http://www.perimeter.org/insourcing

The Journey discipleship curriculum is available through Life on Life Ministries, a ministry of Perimeter Church. This curriculum is designed to assist women and men to become mature and equipped followers of Christ. This curriculum is discipleship based and constructed around five unifying elements—Truth, Equipping, Accountability, Mission, and Supplication—and is structured to offer three unique annual programs of study of twenty-eight weeks each. The inclusive study includes written materials, audio files, leadership video tools, and library topical resources available to all participants. For more information, call 678-405-2238 or visit *http://www.perimeter.org/insourcing.*

Twenty-One Days of Personal Worship

The following presents the daily format for each of the twenty-one days of personal worship. You can print out copies of this form from www.lifeonlife. org/insourcing.

Day _____: Personal Worship

Date: _____ Text: _____

Pray, asking God to forgive specific sins and to speak to you from this passage.

Read the text carefully, noting your observations about the passage.

Ask questions to help you interpret and apply the text to your personal life.

Interpret the passage in a way that is consistent with the teaching of all Scripture.

Summarize a specific and measurable application of the text to your personal life.

By God's grace I will ...
Engage with God in prayer using the five targets of the Lord's Prayer:

1. *God's honor: acknowledging his worth, glory, and majesty.*
   "Our Father in heaven, hallowed is your name."

2. *God's kingdom: acknowledging his priority in the world and in your life.*
   "Your kingdom come, your will be done on earth as it is in heaven."

3. *God's provision: acknowledging his trustworthiness.*
   "Give us this day our daily bread."

4. *God's forgiveness: acknowledging your repentance.*
   "And forgive us our debts, as we also have forgiven our debtors."

5. *God's power: acknowledging your dependence.*
   "And deliver us from the evil one so that we may not be led into temptation."

The Difference between Small Groups and LOLMD Groups

This chart shows some of the distinctives of small groups and LOLMD (Journey) Groups.

Small Groups	LOLMD (Journey) Groups
Knowledge transfer	Life transformation
Leader prepares	Everyone prepares
Low commitment, low cost	High commitment, high cost
Members sign up	Leader selects members
Teach, Pray, Care, Share	Truth, Equipping, Accountability, Mission, Supplication
Size: 8–25	Size: 4–10
Produces community	Produces mature and equipped followers of Christ
Non-Christians and Christians	Christians
Mixed-gender group	Men with men Women with women
Leader is a teacher	Leader is a disciple, coach, mentor
Missional hope	Missional experience
Fellowship	Leader development

Notes

1. "Independence Day: Blowin' Up the White House," accessed February 20, 2012, *http://science.discovery.com/top-ten/2009/science-sfx/science-sfx-9.html*.

2. Alan Hirsch, *The Forgotten Ways: Reactivating the Missional Church* (Grand Rapids, Mich.: Brazos, 2009), 18.

3. "For we are to God the aroma of Christ among those who are being saved and those who are perishing" (2 Cor. 2:15).

4. From A&E's web page for the reality TV show *Intervention*, accessed October 6, 2011, *http://www.aetv.com/intervention/*.

5. I know *discipleship* as a word does not occur in Scripture, but one can argue it is referenced copiously by the word *disciple*.

6. "Self-Described Christians Dominate America but Wrestle with Four Aspects of Spiritual Depth," Barna Group, accessed September 30, 2011, *http://www.barna.org/faith-spirituality/524-self-described-christians-dominate-america-but-wrestle-with-four-aspects-of-spiritual-depth*.

7. Ibid.

8. Michael J. Wilkins, *Following the Master: A Biblical Theology of Discipleship* (Grand Rapids, Mich.: Zondervan, 1992).

9. John Piper, *God's Passion for His Glory: Living the Vision of Jonathan Edwards* (Wheaton, Ill.: Crossway, 2006), 73.

10. Chip Sweney, *A New Kind of Big: How Churches of Any Size Can Partner to Transform Communities* (Grand Rapids, Mich.: Zondervan, 2009), 23.

11. Ibid., 24–25.

12. Used by permission.

13. Drew Harrison and Tom Comyns, "Biomechanics of the Sprint Start," accessed November 11, 2011, *http://www.coachesinfo.com/index.php?option=com_content&id=352&Itemid=181*.

14. Ibid.

15. "Biggest Marathon, Half Marathon Training Mistakes," accessed November 19, 2011, *http://www.sciencedaily.com/releases/2010/02/100226214350.htm*.

16. Coaching videos and other leader materials can be found in the Life on Life section of Perimeter's website, *www.lifeonlife.org/insourcing*.

17. See appendix 1.
18. The version quoted here is ESV.
19. "Bird Flight Explained," BBC News, accessed December 10, 2011, *http://news.bbc.co.uk/2/hi/science/nature/1608251.stm.*
20. See appendix 2 for a table of contents.
21. "'Survivor Tree' Replanted at 9/11 Memorial Plaza," accessed December 15, 2011, *http://abclocal.go.com/wabc/story?section=news/local/new_york&id=7857410.*
22. Matthew 7:21, specifically, life lived in obedience to his words.
23. See *www.lifeonlife.org/insourcing* and *www.perimeter.org/insourcing.*

About Leadership Network

Since 1984, Leadership Network has fostered church innovation and growth by diligently pursuing its far-reaching mission statement: *To identify high-capacity Christian leaders, to connect them with other leaders, and to help them multiply their impact.*

While specific techniques may vary as the church faces new opportunities and challenges, Leadership Network consistently focuses on bringing together entrepreneurial leaders who are pursuing similar ministry initiatives. The resulting peer-to-peer interaction, dialogue, and collaboration—often across denominational lines—helps these leaders better refine their individual strategies and accelerate their own innovations.

To further enhance this process, Leadership Network develops and distributes highly targeted ministry tools and resources, including books, DVDs and videotapes, special reports, e-publications, and free downloads.

For additional information on the mission or activities of Leadership Network, please contact:

Leadership ✖ Network

800-765-5323
www.leadnet.org
client.care@leadnet.org

Leadership Network Innovation Series

Real Stories.
Innovative Ideas.
Transferable
Truths.

How can you fulfill your calling as a ministry leader and help your church experience vitality? Learn from those who have gone before you.

The Leadership Network Innovation Series presents case studies and insights from leading practitioners and pioneering churches that are successfully navigating the ever-changing streams of spiritual renewal in modern society. Each book offers *real* stories about *real* leaders in *real* churches doing *real* ministry.

Bringing It INhouse

Go online to find the resources mentioned in this book as well as additional resources to equip your church in the areas of:

➡ Evangelism
➡ Discipleship
➡ Leadership Development

www.perimeter.org/insourcing

Share Your Thoughts

With the Author: Your comments will be forwarded to
the author when you send them to *zauthor@zondervan.com*.

With Zondervan: Submit your review of this book
by writing to *zreview@zondervan.com*.

Free Online Resources at
www.zondervan.com

Zondervan AuthorTracker: Be notified whenever your favorite
authors publish new books, go on tour, or post an update
about what's happening in their lives at www.zondervan.com/
authortracker.

Daily Bible Verses and Devotions: Enrich your life with daily
Bible verses or devotions that help you start every morning
focused on God. Visit www.zondervan.com/newsletters.

Free Email Publications: Sign up for newsletters on Christian
living, academic resources, church ministry, fiction, children's
resources, and more. Visit www.zondervan.com/newsletters.

Zondervan Bible Search: Find and compare Bible passages in
a variety of translations at www.zondervanbiblesearch.com.

Other Benefits: Register to receive online benefits like
coupons and special offers, or to participate in research.

ZONDERVAN.com/
AUTHORTRACKER
follow your favorite authors